Praise

Sara Jewell is a born storyteller and her snarp-witted but kind-hearted portraits of country people, places, and customs make for a remarkable first book....A welcome new voice in Atlantic Canadian literature.
—**Harry Thurston**, author of *A Place Between the Tides* and *The Deer Yard*

Charming, brave, and spiritually refreshing, *Field Notes* is a love song to the country and all the humans and creatures who make their lives there. City-raised Sara Jewell's essays present a resonant array of subjects and themes, all compulsively readable and deftly explored. A funny and touching tribute to small rural communities, and the vibrant realities therein.
—**Marjorie Simmins**, author of *Coastal Lives* and *Year of the Horse*

What a delightful book this is! Some readers will want this book to revisit favourite columns, and others—like myself—will discover this good-hearted writer for the first time and feel as if they've made a new friend.

In her warm, often wry voice, Sara Jewell speaks clearly and directly, interspersing intimate revelations about her own life with pertinent personal stories of other Maritimers. In a gentle and thoughtful way, she touches on a variety of topics and gathers us into her own conversation with the natural world, allowing us to see it through her eyes. Couldn't be better.
—**Isabel Huggan**, author of *The Elizabeth Stories* and *Belonging: Home Away From Home*

Sara Jewell's heart is firmly rooted in rural Nova Scotia: its landscape and its people. In *Field Notes,* a lively cast of characters helps Jewell learn about life, love, and belonging. Through them and their stories, she learns what it means to be—finally—at home.
—**Pam Chamberlain**, editor of *Country Roads: Memoirs from Rural Canada*

Within the pages of *Field Notes* I found a soul sister. Sara Jewell digs, with tenderness and wisdom, into the rich loam of life that nourishes rural Atlantic Canada. Delivered with gentle humour and prose as clear and lilting as the song of the hermit thrush at dusk, her thoughtful reflections and observations remind us of the harvest of healing we reap when people, landscapes, and creatures find harmony.
—**Deborah Carr**, author of *Sanctuary: The Story of Naturalist Mary Majka*

A thoughtful and engaging examination of rural Nova Scotia (and life in general) that rings with the conviction that, yes, you can go back, in order to move forward. Jewell digs through moving tales of elephants and hair stylists, trees and ticks, dogs, babies, and octogenarians to reach the marrow of the universal human concerns about life, death, change, tradition, work, friendship—and mostly: love.
—**Monica Graham**, author of *In the Spirit: Reflections on Everyday Grace*

Field Notes

Field Notes

*A City Girl's Search for Heart and Home
in Rural Nova Scotia*

*Marg,
from my heart to yours!*

SARA JEWELL

Sara ♡

NIMBUS
PUBLISHING LTD

Nimbus Publishing Limited
3731 Mackintosh St, Halifax, NS B3K 5A5
(902) 455-4286 nimbus.ca

Printed and bound in Canada

NB1258

Cover design: Heather Bryan
Interior design: Jenn Embree
Cover photo: Catherine Bussiere
All drawings © Joanna Close

Previous versions of some of these essays have appeared in other publications, including: the *Oxford Journal*, the *Citizen-Record*, the *Chronicle-Herald*, *Saltscapes*
magazine, the *United Church Observer*, and the *Women in Nature* anthology.

Library and Archives Canada Cataloguing in Publication
    Jewell, Sara, author
    Field notes : a city girl's search for heart and home in rural
    Nova Scotia / Sara Jewell.
    Issued in print and electronic formats.
    ISBN 978-1-77108-419-2 (paperback).—ISBN 978-1-77108-420-8 (html)
1. Country life—Nova Scotia—Pugwash—Anecdotes. 2. Pugwash (N.S.)—
Anecdotes. I. Title.

FC2349.P83J49 2016   971.6'11   C2016-903740-1
                                   C2016-903741-X

Nimbus Publishing acknowledges the financial support for its publishing activities from the Government of Canada through the Canada Book Fund (CBF)
and the Canada Council for the Arts, and from the Province of Nova Scotia. We
are pleased to work in partnership with the Province of Nova Scotia to develop
and promote our creative industries for the benefit of all Nova Scotians.

Out beyond ideas of rightdoing and wrongdoing, there is a field.

I'll meet you there.

—Rumi

Contents

One Hundred Thousand Welcomes 1

Blessed Be the Ties that Bind 9

1. A River Runs Through Him - - - - - - - - - 10
2. That's What Friends are for - - - - - - - - - 16
3. The Medallions - - - - - - - - - - - - 22
4. The Secrets of a Long and Happy Marriage - - - - 27
5. Must Love Dogs - - - - - - - - - - - - 33
6. My Husband Knows Jack About Decorating - - - - 38
7. Hobgoblins - - - - - - - - - - - - 44
8. Nanny and Grampie Get an iPad - - - - - - - 49
9. The Artist's Way - - - - - - - - - - - 54
10. The Journey of Granny's Chest - - - - - - - 60

Life is Short: Live in the Country 65

1. Starry, Starry Night - - - - - - - - - - 66
2. The Americans Have Arrived - - - - - - - - 71
3. Shit (and the Weather) Happens - - - - - - - 76
4. Give Us This Day Our Daily Egg - - - - - - - 82
5. A Country Woman Carries On - - - - - - - - 87
6. Faith in the Community - - - - - - - - - 94
7. By Any Other Name - - - - - - - - - - 100
8. Good Vibrations - - - - - - - - - - - 106
9. Check Me for Ticks - - - - - - - - - - 111
10. It'll be All Right - - - - - - - - - - 116
11. A Hot Time in the Old Town - - - - - - - 120

The Country Lives of Animals — 125

1. City Dog, Country Dog — 126
2. The Blessing of the Ospreys — 132
3. Communion With the Livestock — 138
4. Rescue Me — 144
5. The Truth About Roadkill — 150
6. Three O'clock in the Morning — 154
7. Funeral for a Mouse — 160
8. Deer to my Heart — 165
9. The Face of Timeless Devotion — 170
10. Ma'am, Back Away From the Goats — 176

The Rural Appreciation Society — 183

1. A Farm Education — 184
2. Ghosts in Our Machines — 190
3. A Walk in the Woods — 195
4. The Rural Wavelength — 200
5. Learning to Drive, Country Style — 205
6. Muslims in the Maritimes — 210
7. What Future Does a Tree Have? — 215
8. More Power to Them — 220
9. The Inevitable End of Summer — 226
10. Recipe for a Maritime Dinner Party — 231

Acknowledgements — 237

One Hundred
Thousand
Welcomes

$\mathcal{W}$hen I was twenty-six years old and newly married, I left Ontario and moved to Vancouver. It was the mid-nineties, before the new millennium, before the internet was part of our daily lives, and before there was even caller ID. I quickly found work as a radio newscaster. When Swissair 111 crashed into the ocean off the coast of Nova Scotia in 1997, I remember feeling far more connected to the event than anyone else in my circle of friends.

We had the usual busy lives of twentysomethings living in a city: finishing grad school, starting careers, getting married, buying homes, meeting new people through work, play, and parties. One unique detail bonded us together: most of us had arrived on the west coast from somewhere else. Some came from as close as Kamloops and others as far away as Truro. Perhaps a handful were born and raised in Vancouver, but most of us were come-from-aways. It didn't seem to matter to anyone since Vancouver was a young city—cosmopolitan, temperate, and easygoing. It was a place people chose to move to.

"So, where are you from?" was the go-to opening line for any conversation.

Ten years later and four time zones to the east, it's a whole different world: older, more established, and deeply rooted. For a region that celebrates its Scottish and British roots and can claim a geological affiliation with Africa, it seems its inhabitants take the question of where you are from very seriously, as if they are waiting to stick one of those red-ended tacks into the spot on the map of Atlantic Canada where you were born.

On the east coast, the first question always seems to be, "Who are your parents?" because in the Maritimes, it's assumed you were lucky enough to be born and raised here. With that assumption underlying all greetings, what matters isn't where you came from but *who* you came from: it is your family name that places you and gives your existence context. "Who are your parents?" and the subsequent answer is considered almost as essential as food, shelter and, you know, *oxygen*.

I have to admit, it's a habit that both intrigues and discomfits me. I'm not the type to ask personal questions of someone I've just met, nor does it occur to me to want to know who someone's parents are. I can appreciate, however, that meeting me might frustrate the average Maritimer; with my "mysterious" past, no one knows immediately where (or who) I came from. I may have married into a local family with deep roots but when someone asks, "Who was she before she married Dwayne?" the answer will be, "Sara Jewell," or worse: "I don't know." Since my birth name won't ring a bell, the next question must be, "Well, who were her parents?" The answer to that is, "Reg and Lynda Jewell," or worse: "I don't know."

By asking, "Where is she from?" the person will be hoping to receive some kind of information to help place me in the giant family tree that is Nova Scotia. The answer will prove unhelpful: "She's from Ontario." I am a mystery woman without a past, without a local family, and without roots everyone has been tripping over for at least five generations. No one knows who my family is and where we fit in. It makes us appear to not fit in at all.

But we do. There *is* a lineage here for my family. We may not be able to claim multiple generations on the same land or a homestead dating back to the 1700s, but we did put down roots. They run close to the surface but they are there, eagerly grasping for a hold in this red soil.

I know. I've been cleaning that dirt off the bottom of my father's car since I was nine years old.

My husband has lived in the house he built for more than thirty-five years, a house located half a kilometre down the road from where he was raised. By contrast, I've collected a lot of addresses: sixteen in total, including two in Toronto where I was born, three in the town of Cobourg, Ontario, (which I consider my hometown), four during university in Kingston, Ontario, and four in Vancouver, British Columbia. For a family that was not connected with the military, a circus, or fraud, we moved a lot. Yet there was one constant throughout the thirty-six years before I met my husband: Pugwash Point Road, Nova Scotia.

I was nine years old when my family came to Nova Scotia for the first time. We arrived for a holiday on the invitation of our minister, Garth Mundle, back in Cobourg; he spent his summer in the place where he was born and raised and he wanted to share his cabin on the back shore with his friends. He wanted us to experience what kept drawing him back to Pugwash with his own family.

Pugwash is the anglicized version of the original Mi'kmaw, *Pagweak,* which means "deep water." The small fishing village about an hour from the New Brunswick border is tucked around a narrow harbour that opens up onto the Northumberland Strait. Salt boats regularly ease their way through the twisting channel to retrieve their loads from the salt mine, while lobster fishers motor in and out of the harbour. Farms, home, and cottages dot the red shore.

Each August, we would drive through this village to reach our minister's rustic cabin located in a back field of his brother's dairy farm, perched on the edge of a cliff overlooking the Northumberland Strait. Nothing but deep blue water, bright blue sky, green fields, and red soil surrounded us—it was such a piece of heaven we didn't mind the lack of running water and electricity. The outhouse squatted partway down the cliff amid wild rose bushes, and that somehow made the whole place seem even more exotic.

Because of the enthusiastic welcome we received from both Garth and his family (and from his younger brother, Eldon, and his family), this became our annual summer holiday. Year after year in August, just as haying season ended, we arrived at the back shore of Pugwash Point to stay at Garth's cabin and soak up the last of the summer sunshine. In later years, we stayed at Eldon's farm where my sister, Araminta, and I trailed after Eldon's two red-haired daughters, trying to be farm girls ourselves. My father fit in perfectly; the men and the village reminded him of his childhood. My mother was perfectly content anywhere as long as she could read, shop, and eat—there wasn't a local cookbook or handmade quilt she didn't bring back to Ontario at the end of our vacations. We rarely went a week the rest of the year without a mention of Pugwash.

Once Araminta and I started university and stopped going east, however, my parents felt they'd imposed on Garth and Eldon's hospitality long enough. "We either buy our own place or we stop coming," Dad said in August 1995. That's when the old Seaman place near the end of the road came up for sale.

◦ · ◦

The geography of Vancouver wasn't so different from that of our little corner of Nova Scotia. On the west coast, there were mountains (only larger), an ocean (the Pacific), a strait (Georgia), and a big island on the horizon (Vancouver). When my dog, Maggie, and I spent Saturday mornings walking the beach along English Bay, our route was dictated by whether the tide was in or out. Familiar black-and-red freighters lined up in the bay. There were crabs and clams and salmon for supper. Whales and seals played in the water while bald eagles soared overhead. Yet I longed for something else.

These weren't the seals sunning themselves on a shoal of rocks at the back shore near Garth's cabin. That sand was too brown. Those freighters weren't navigating a narrow, sandbar-clogged harbour. The sun wasn't as hot, the water wasn't as cold, and those Atlantic lobsters spent two days getting to Granville Island Market.

After they purchased the Seaman place, my parents started spending June through August in Nova Scotia—four time zones away. There was math involved when one of us wanted to pick up the phone for a chat. Sometimes, when I mentioned having to phone my parents in Nova Scotia, a person would ask if I was from there. I always wanted to say yes. Yet it never occurred to me that I would see the east coast ever again. My memories were strong and vibrant, but they felt firmly fixed in the past; I was too wrapped up in my life to recognize the quiet tugging on my heart.

During the five years I lived in Vancouver, I filled two photo albums with pictures of Pugwash Point: sunsets, cows, the house, the long wildflower-filled lane, the harbour, and the salt boats. When my mother sent mail from Nova Scotia, the envelopes arrived thick with photographs of a place I hadn't visited in ten years.

One morning as I was walking Maggie along the beach, I found a large sand dollar. I took it home and propped it up on the mantel in the living room so I could sit and look at it. I wondered how many sand dollars I would need to buy a plane ticket to Nova Scotia.

In 2001, the life I'd established in Vancouver collapsed. When my husband told me he didn't want to be married any longer, I didn't call a lawyer, talk to my minister, or even tell my best friend. My first thought—and only plan—was *go to Pugwash*. Some deeply rooted instinct knew whatever I'd hoped to find through marriage and work on the west coast wasn't attainable there. I was on the wrong side of the country.

I headed east to the one place—the only place—I wanted to be. I needed to regroup and reconnect with the person who went missing long before she'd headed to the big city. Those years of searching for my place in the world led me right back to the red gravel roads. My first kiss happened in Nova Scotia, in a horse barn on a hot August night when I was twelve years old. You don't forget your first kiss; you don't forget where it happened. You don't lose a connection like that. Perhaps this was my first inkling of the pull Maritimers feel to their land and shore.

I stopped coming to Nova Scotia with my parents when I was eighteen. When I returned at the age of thirty-two, it was to live with my parents to help take care of my father who had been diagnosed with dementia. This meant spending four months of every year at the summer home they now owned on Pugwash Point Road. That's when I found true devotion and commitment: first with my parents, then later with a Nova Scotia country boy. It was not the one who kissed me when I was twelve, but one who kissed me when I was thirty-six on the front porch of that summer house on a hot July night. You don't forget a kiss like that. And you don't lose that connection a second time.

How many of us get a chance to experience it all over again? To do as an adult all the things you didn't know you wanted when you were nine, eighteen, twenty-six? To take everything that was familiar and meaningful—everything you thought was important—and allow your heart to show you a whole new set of possibilities?

They say you can never go back but they are wrong.

Blessed Be the Ties that Bind

1

A River Runs Through Him

------ · ·· ------

I married a man with a river running through his veins. My husband grew up on a farm on the shores of the narrow, winding River Philip; a tidal river that begins in the Cobequid Mountains above Williamsdale, Nova Scotia, and stretches more than thirty-two kilometres, flowing past Collingwood and Oxford, to the Northumberland Strait at Port Howe/Port Philip.

"I love that river," Dwayne says after nearly six decades with it at his doorstep. "I loved it when we were fishing it, swimming in it, and in the wintertime, skating on it and hauling wood over it."

When I listen to him tell his stories about the river, I can sense how well he knows it. In any season, he knows how it will behave and what to expect from it, as if this part-salt, part-freshwater river undulating through his tiny portion of the world is as essential as the blood coursing through his body. The wisdom gained from a lifetime along its shores flows through him, as do the memories.

"When we got snowmobiles in the sixties, the river was a highway," he recalls. "I remember in the evenings, after chores, going down to check out all the guys who were fishing smelts through the ice. It was like a little village with the gaslights hanging on the poles holding the nets."

Dwayne's instinctive feel for the river was instilled through his paternal grandfather, Floyd Mattinson: a small-statured, deeply religious, hard-working carpenter. During the winter, after supper and chores, Floyd sat in his rocking chair over the register above the furnace and passed the long, dark evenings telling stories. As a boy sitting in his grandparents' warm kitchen, Dwayne absorbed everything, particularly the story of how his grandfather came to settle the family on the river.

"When Grampie was ten years old, he would leave his home in Mount Pleasant and walk down to the River Philip," Dwayne explains. "That would be five miles. He'd have his gun and his dog with him and he'd be gone for three or four days, hunting partridge and rabbit. Then he found this point of land on the river and when he returned home, he told his parents that some day he would live down there."

Floyd Mattinson finally made good on that vow and bought the fifty-four-acre point, which came with a house and two barns, in August 1920. He was already married to Margaret MacKay, a school-teacher in Mount Pleasant, who was pregnant with the first of their three children.

"We grew up calling it Orchard Point because Grampie planted forty apple trees alongside his house," Dwayne says. "A lot of them were still there when I was a kid. Part of the old orchard is still there now."

Floyd died in the fall of 1973 at age eighty, and his wife Margaret followed him that November. Of their three children, my father-in-law, Donn, is the only one who stayed on the farm, shifting the small operation from dairy to beef and moving another house onto the property for his wife, Mary, and the three children they would eventually have. Born in 1925, Donn's childhood memories are of a long-lost way of life.

"The river was used for transportation in the horse-and-sled days because the road wasn't plowed then," he remembers. "They used the river, when it froze, to go to Oxford for groceries and to haul wood with horses and sleds."

But that was the practical use of the river; for children and young people, it offered a plethora of activities and adventures, particularly in winter. According to Donn, Orchard Point itself was a natural gathering spot.

"It's good and straight along here and handy to the house," he says. "Kids from Port Howe would skate here and we'd have a great bonfire. You could skate right into the shore around the banks where an old tree had fallen down and two or three of us would grab a hold of it and break it off and drag it down to the fire. It was some nice to have a fire to skate around and get warmed up."

Donn's grandmother was still alive in the 1930s, living with Floyd and Margaret and the kids. He fondly remembers his Gran and Mother making what he calls "a god-awful amount of fudge."

"We'd all crowd in the house," he says, "and I think sometimes we'd have a bit of music and a dance."

Donn was greatly influenced by what he experienced as a boy and what he learned. For him, the river was a source of food in the summer, a method of transportation in the winter, and a means to support a family year-round. Donn made sure to carry on those traditions when his own sons, Dwayne and Adair, were young. The brothers were the third generation of Mattinson men to work the family's three-hundred-acre woodlot across the river.

"My first memory of the river is hauling wood across the ice with Dad," my husband recalls. "I was six or seven years old. Not likely doing a lot but I was there. It's in my blood to go to the woods on a Saturday to cut wood."

As families move away from rural areas and fewer people find employment in agriculture and forestry, there are skills, experiences, knowledge, and stories disappearing. When the boys first started going to the river with their father and grandfather, they used horses and sleds to haul the timber out of the woodlot and across the ice, but by the sixties, a tractor replaced the horses.

"It didn't matter how cold it was, you went to the woods," Dwayne says. "I remember one morning when I was fourteen, I don't know how cold it was but it was as cold as hell. Neither Adair nor I wanted to go. When we got across the river to the woodlot, the power saw wouldn't start because it was so damn cold. Dad changed the spark plugs and wires and tried heating the carburetor up with a lighter. It wouldn't start and I kept thinking, 'Don't start!' because I wanted to go home."

He got his wish. In the end, the power saw didn't start because Donn got so frustrated, "he grabbed the saw by the blade with a pair of leather pullovers he was wearing and beat it against a tree and smashed it all to hell," Dwayne chuckles at the memory.

Whether boating or snowmobiling, Dwayne says he has never been afraid of the river because of the knowledge passed down from father to son, grandfather to grandson; knowledge that saved their lives in the spring of 1977.

"It had been a good winter, lots of snow and ice," Dwayne remembers. "But it was April and it was mild. You'd go to the woods in the morning and it would be cold but by eleven o'clock, you only had on a T-shirt and pants, no cap or gloves."

Dwayne explains when the ice goes "bad" in the river it means there are soft spots where you could fall through. The telltale sign is when the ice turns grey. That's what they noticed on that April morning: "We took a load home at noon and ate our dinner and unloaded. Going back, Dad said we would bring the gear back because we were done. 'She's going out,' he said about the ice."

Twenty-four hours later, the ice was gone.

"I knew it was getting bad and so did Dad," Dwayne says. "That was close. In front of Grampie's house, the river is over fifty feet deep. That's a lot of water if you go through the ice on a tractor."

Dwayne's stories connect him to this space—this stretch of river, farmland, and woods in northern Nova Scotia—where he was born and raised. I listen and learn, absorbing the details, knowing I'll never experience the river the way he did. Even though I live here now, the river will never be a part of me the way it is part of my husband. As an adult and a newcomer, I relate to the river as a view out my car windows as I drive along the paved highway. My contact with it is occasional, paddling a canoe or throwing sticks into the water for the dog.

My greatest disappointment is that I won't get the chance to skate on the river in the winter. After ninety years living along the river, Donn says the biggest change he's seen is that it doesn't freeze the same.

"It never freezes as hard or [for] as long as it used to," Donn explains. "Back when I was a kid, it froze over in November and it stayed that way until April."

Dwayne believes the biggest change has come from the herbicides and pesticides sprayed on the blueberry fields up in the mountain where the River Philip begins.

"That grass that's growing all over the river? It wasn't there twenty years ago. It wasn't even that bad when I was snowmobiling all the time in 2004. There was the odd spot you had to watch because there'd be a bump when the tide was out but the river is just loaded with grass now."

A lot has changed since Floyd Mattinson coveted that point of land on the river in 1904. With his two sons holding down full-time, off-farm jobs, Donn sold the last of his cattle in 1992. Even though his sons now co-own the big woodlot across the river where they worked as boys, it hasn't been logged for personal use in ten years.

"I miss the exercise and the fresh air," my husband admits. "I miss hanging out with my father."

After hearing these stories of the river, I ask my mother-in-law if she has any photos. A few days later, Dwayne returns from visiting his parents with an envelope. When he opens it, half a dozen photographs spill out onto the dining room table. Dwayne picks up a black-and-white photo of himself as a young boy standing next to the family's first snowmobile.

"I was ten years old," he says. That would make it 1966.

He picks up another one, this one in colour.

"Wow," is all he says. In the photo, he is standing next to a snow-mobile with *King of the Road* emblazoned on the nose. "Eighteen-horsepower Olympic, single cylinder," he murmurs. "Wow."

He is perfectly still as he studies the photo.

"My father gave me a snowmobile," he says eventually. "It was Christmas morning. I was fourteen. Along with all the other knick-knacks and candy in my stocking was a note telling me to look on the verandah. It was a snowmobile just for me."

As he looks at the photos and tells me more stories about growing up on the farm at Orchard Point, I sense that not only is the river a part of him but it is a part of an entire line of men. They were shaped by a way of life that is quietly retreating into memories shared by an old man sitting in a rocking chair with his grandson on his knee.

"You don't realize how lucky you are," Dwayne says.

2

That's What Friends Are For

*I*n my favourite photo of Diana and me, we stand with our arms around each other. Her golden retriever, Clancy, leans against our legs. It was taken a few months after she'd had surgery to remove tumours from her esophagus and I'd started dating a Nova Scotia country boy—we both look happy.

The photo always reminds me of what she said after she was back in her small white house on Pugwash Point: "I'm away having major surgery because I have cancer and what do you do? Fall in love!" Hey, that's what friends are for.

It's remarkable that if it hadn't been for our two pups, Diana and I would never have met, let alone become friends. Early one morning in September, with only a few weeks left in my summer on Pugwash Point, I walked with my eighteen-month-old boxer, Stella, towards the end of the Point Road where I would turn around and head back home.

We'd walked by the white house on the corner hundreds of times, yet on that particular morning, a year-old golden retriever named Clancy bounded out to greet us. After a few mornings of Stella and Clancy playing in his yard, Diana stepped out the door and asked if she could walk with us.

As simple as that, a city girl and a country girl became friends.

Two years later, in the middle of the first summer we weren't spending at our house in Nova Scotia because of the progression of my father's dementia and my mother's recent cancer diagnosis, I got the call about Diana. I packed up my car and headed east. Of course I'd drive sixteen hundred kilometres to see her before her surgery. That's what friends are for. And Diana wasn't just any friend.

When I was in Ontario, this was the woman I proudly called my "Nova Scotia friend." When I was on Pugwash Point, this was the woman I met at the end of the lane at six o'clock every morning. This was the mother of Clancy, Stella's best friend. This was the woman who provided the best shampoo for washing Stella after her frequent run-ins with skunks, who told me stories about growing up in Cape Breton, drank tea on our front porch, and always beat me at Scrabble. She took me to my first—and only—Bingo night, and became my regular movie buddy from the night we saw—what else?—*Must Love Dogs*.

We may have become friends because of our dogs but going to the movies with Diana defined and deepened our friendship in a new way. Driving to the theatre took an hour each way, on winding roads through Wentworth Valley and over Folly Mountain. For an entire hour, it was just Diana and me with no distractions, no dementia-related crisis or neighbours interrupting our conversation. We were free to talk about anything we wanted, and I allowed this time with Diana to be my distraction from my caregiving duties. On the way to the theatre, we'd chat about the dogs, books, country music videos, and her three grown children. "I'm not much of a chatterbox," Diana once said to me, "but you don't seem to notice."

Less than a year after my favourite photo was taken, just six months after my wedding, Diana received bad news. When I walked into her kitchen on a cold February afternoon, the first thing I noticed was Clancy's weight gain. He had filled out, which meant he was getting most of Diana's food and not many walks—she was in too much pain to go very far. As Diana poured our tea, I noticed she was thin again, like she had been before the first tumours were removed. As we talked, Clancy rested his head on her lap and Diana rubbed his ears.

"I'm shocked at how quickly the cancer came back," Diana admitted, although she'd been told there was an 85 percent chance it would return within five years. "One day I was fine, then I started going downhill."

She'd refused treatment after the surgery, not wanting to be sick through Christmas, but now she was going to have radiation in an attempt to shrink the new tumour.

"How are you feeling?" I asked after half an hour. "Do you want me to leave?"

"I'm getting tired," Diana answered, "but it's nice to have company."

Before her radiation treatments began, we headed to the theatre for our monthly movie date and saw *P.S. I Love You*. After the trailer for *Mamma Mia* played, I leaned over to Diana and whispered, "We're going to see that when it comes out in July!" As I sat back, I was horrified: I'd just made a date six months in the future with a woman battling an aggressive cancer. What if I jinxed her?

Our drives to and from the theatre had taken on a new importance after Diana was diagnosed. For those one-hour interludes, I was her distraction, her "cancer-free zone," in which we talked about everything but her health. On this particular night, however, the ride home was different. As we drove along inside the dark, warm car, the engine droning and a white moon shining above the black woods on either side of the road, it was Diana who did all the talking. With radiation looming, she shared what was on her mind.

"This treatment will buy me time and make me more comfortable," she said. Her daughter, Angela, was upset that her mother had not held a grandchild yet. "I told her there was no point in trying to change that fact now," Diana said. As we passed the silent, black stain of Folly Lake, Diana wondered out loud what the point of her fifty-four years had been.

Silence fell between us. If I could have spoken without crying, I would have answered her question. In hindsight, I should have worried less about upsetting Diana with my tears and more about her hearing my words. I would have told her that our three-year friendship changed my life. The only way I knew how to make sense of Diana's disease—and her life—was in my own context: her diagnosis brought me to where I was supposed to be. If Diana hadn't had surgery that summer, I wouldn't have rushed east to see her before she left for the hospital. I wouldn't have said yes to that blind date. If I hadn't met and married Dwayne, I wouldn't have been here to drive her to the movies for a laugh, sometimes a cry, and a long chat.

We may have become friends because of our dogs but it was our personalities that bonded us quickly and deeply, as if whatever force introduced us on that September morning knew we had to cram what would have been a long friendship into only a few years. Where I was energetic and chatty, Diana was calm and quiet, full of Cape Breton pragmatism. She'd say, "Don't talk so foolish," and I'd laugh while taking her words to heart. We saw each other every day for four months of the year, creating a connection that was short in duration but strong in meaning and memories. Even if Diana had lived another twenty years, I would never forget every moment we spent together during my summers on Pugwash Point.

Diana didn't make it to our first wedding anniversary party at the end of July. She was in the hospital finding out the reason she couldn't breathe was the liquid around her heart, and learning that her prognosis was now between two and twenty months. In the middle of preparing food for the party, I stopped to write a long letter to Diana, thanking her for being such a big part of my happiness. I added, "As soon as you're having a good day, we must go to the movies."

A week after the party, Diana called. "I'm having a good day," she said. "Let's go tonight."

Six hours later, we were sitting in a darkened movie theatre, eating popcorn and watching *Mamma Mia*. I concentrated on my intense gratitude for this moment, not on the too-obvious fact that there weren't many more of these evenings to come.

A couple of months later, I was working at my computer on a Saturday morning when I thought about calling Diana to see if she was up for a matinee. My hand was on the receiver but then I thought of the deadlines I was facing and how much I could get accomplished by staying home. I didn't make the call.

Later that day, the phone rang.

"Diana's gone," her husband, Matt, choked out.

In that small white house in the first curve of the Pugwash Point Road, my dear friend had dropped to the floor of her living room just after lunch, downed by a massive heart attack. As it turned out, Diana had exactly two months to live.

Thoughts pinged around my brain: If only I had called her! She might have died in my car! I thought we had more time! Who would I go to the movies with now?

The next morning, my husband suggested a four-wheeler drive through our three-hundred-acre woodlot on the other side of the river. "You can sit there and cry when you need to," he said. When I shoved my hands into the pockets of my jacket to pull out a pair of gloves, I also pulled out a small piece of paper. It was the ticket stub for *P.S. I Love You,* the movie Diana and I had seen in March.

"You were such a good friend to her," Matt said as we hugged before the funeral.

Yet I was tormented by questions: Was I a good enough friend? Why didn't I visit more? Why didn't I go over for more games of Scrabble? Why didn't I call that morning? My rational side reminded me that Diana hadn't been able to walk very far and the medication made her groggy. I remembered how she hadn't been able to laugh during *Mamma Mia* because it made her cough, and coughing made her gag. I remembered Matt and Diana had been at our place for supper just two weeks before she died.

"You were a good friend," my husband assured me. "You went to the movies all the time." But now that she was gone, it didn't seem like enough. Knowing she'd died the way she'd wanted to—at home, not in pain, not suffering in hospital—did not diminish my regret. I wished I'd bought her a pair of really cute pyjamas.

Two weeks after the funeral, I stopped at the bank machine in Pugwash and when I took my hand out of my pocket to shove my bank card into the machine, there was a small piece of white paper stuck to my palm.

It was the ticket stub for *Mamma Mia*.

I'd used this card many times since we'd seen that movie in August. I certainly hadn't been wearing this wool coat that summer evening. I had no idea where that stub came from and didn't even recall keeping it. It simply appeared in my hand on this day when I was missing Diana, wanting to drive to her house for a cup of tea, and wishing for the millionth time I'd been a better friend.

"Don't talk so foolish," she'd say to me now. I still miss her calmness, her quiet sense of humour, her ruthlessness at Scrabble. I miss my Nova Scotia friend. That favourite picture of Diana and me is tucked into the frame around the mirror in my bedroom and next to it are those two ticket stubs. They belong together, that photo of a country girl and a city girl, and the memories of the last two movies we saw together. They belong together like a pair of dogs running through muddy ditches in the morning sun and the two women walking on the road, laughing.

3

The Medallions

When I moved into my husband's home, one of our first chores was to clean out the basement, which had mostly become a storage space for stuff his ex-wife had left behind. A couple of boxes, however, contained his own mementos, which were getting musty in the cool, damp basement. In one of his boxes, I found a set of dog tags on a chain, round and old, stamped with *Christena J. MacDonald, Nurse, A.N.C. Base Hosp No. 6. U.S.A.*

"Those medallions belonged to my Aunt Jean," my husband said. "Don't throw them out."

As if I would. And if they were that important, they certainly deserved a better home than a musty box in the basement. I dropped them into a small white jeweller's box and tucked it into the top drawer of his dresser. A few years later, while looking for our passports, I came across the box. This time, I wanted to know who Christena MacDonald was and why my husband had her dog tags. I called my mother-in-law.

"Oh, you mean Aunt Jean," Mary said. "My father had three sisters and Jean was one of them. She was a nurse in Boston, and she went to the front lines in France, I think. All of my aunts were nurses and none them married."

As my writer's brain pinged with disappointment that there weren't any children to share the story of their mother's nursing career, Mary said, "Did I ever tell you that I lost a child? He was stillborn."

"No," I breathed.

"He came after Beverley. He's the reason we have Dwayne."

Then I remembered that yes, I'd heard about a baby that didn't live. One of the first stories Dwayne ever told me was about flipping his father's 1969 Chevy pickup onto its roof while driving home in a snowstorm when he was sixteen. He stayed at a friend's house that night and they'd pulled the truck out early the next morning with a tractor in order to get Dwayne home in time to do the chores.

"Dad had looked the truck over and there wasn't a scratch on it but I knew I was in trouble," he said. "I wanted to get out of there but he said to me, 'You gotta eat breakfast.' We sat there at the table and Dad didn't say a word to me, he just looked at Mum and said, 'Mary, I wonder how the other fella would've turned out.'"

My husband laughed when he told this story, got a kick out of it, having been the hellraiser son who worked hard but played harder. Yet all he knows about the brother who died was his father's comment—the punchline of his story.

There was more to the story, and my mother-in-law was willing to tell me. When Mary married Donn in 1948, she became a farmer's wife, moving from her parents' home in Bayhead, (between Wallace and Tatamagouche along the Northumberland Strait), to a farm eighty kilometres away along the River Philip. Her husband had dairy cows, a woodlot, and a gravel truck. Donn worked hard but money was tight so they didn't own a car, just borrowed his parents' or his Aunt Martha's, who lived eleven kilometres away in Oxford.

The house was Mary's domain. In it, she raised three children, cooked three meals a day, and fed any men working for them.

She cooked with a wood stove, baking eighteen loaves of bread a week along with pies, roasts, potatoes, and other seasonable vegetables. Winter or summer, the wood stove was always warm.

Now, sitting in my living room with the phone pressed against my ear, I listened as Mary told me the whole story about the son she lost. It was 1954 and she was pregnant with her third child. She had gone to the hospital in Tatamagouche for her first two births but since those had gone smoothly, she'd planned a home birth for her third child. Since her own mother had died two years earlier at the age of fifty, her Aunt Jean was coming to stay for the birth. During this pregnancy, however, Mary had developed phlebitis, a painful swelling of the legs caused by blood clots. Aunt Jean came a month early to take care of Mary and the two older children, aged five and three.

"It had been a difficult day," Mary told me about September 23. "I was eight months pregnant and my father was very sick. I'd been down to see him in Bayhead and then come home to bake pies to feed the threshers the next day." A grain-threshing crew was usually ten to twelve men. That evening, she started to bleed and cramp. She thought it might be false labour but when the symptoms worsened, Aunt Jean called the doctor.

"He stayed until he realized I wasn't in labour," Mary remembered. "It wasn't time for the baby to be born and he didn't know there was anything wrong. There were no tests or machines then. We had no ultrasounds. Back then, you either had a child or you didn't."

Since the closest hospital was a forty-five-minute drive over dirt roads and Donn's parents had taken their car to Halifax, Mary stayed in bed.

"I didn't sleep at all. I had pain all night. Daylight had come when I started hemorrhaging."

Donn called his aunt to bring her car but the doctor arrived first. Mary was bleeding so heavily, a long streak of red marked the wall as her husband carried her downstairs to the doctor's car.

"I was in the back seat of the car with blankets and towels all packed around me," she said. "Aunt Jean sat in the front and Donn had to wait for his aunt. But we didn't get further than the bideau."

Where the river widens and the road narrows on the road now known as Route 301, the pavement was laid over a large wooden culvert. It was always called the Simpson Dyke but long-time locals refer to it as "the bideau," their pronunciation of the Acadian word *aboiteau*. The bideau is a mere kilometre from Donn and Mary's home.

"I told the doctor I was having contractions. I said, 'Stop! The baby is coming.' Aunt Jean was out of the car first and she caught the baby."

Mary stopped talking. She didn't speak for a long time.

"I remember the sound of the road grader going by," she finally said. Her voice had become thick and soft, and then she began to weep.

This loss was not buried deeply; it remained close to the surface, thin and translucent like ice on the river in December. One step and she broke through, falling into the cold water of grief.

Eventually, Mary carried on with the story.

"They drove me home and Aunt Jean brought the baby inside the house. She wrapped him in towels and laid him on the open door of the wood stove where it was warm. She was trying to revive him but she couldn't. He was gone." The sadness in her voice is decades old. "He's buried up in the cemetery," said Mary, "but there is no name on the headstone because the doctor told me that stillborn babies weren't named. Every year on his birthday, September 24, I put roses on his grave."

The doctor also told her the problem was *placenta previa*, when the placenta covers the cervical opening. This condition would be detected today during a routine ultrasound. Even though Mary couldn't see my face, I wiped tears away and swallowed a couple of times before I dared asked a question.

"Did you have a name picked out?"

"Dwayne Jonathan," Mary answered promptly. "I didn't tell anyone. He was buried without a name but in my heart, he was Dwayne."

But that's my husband's name.

"The doctor said I shouldn't have any other children on account of the phlebitis but Donn wanted another boy," Mary told me.

Back then, women lived so much closer to life and death—*you either had a child or you didn't*—and there was no time for mourning, no time to regret the decision of a home birth. There was a husband

and hired hands to feed, there were other children to care for, another child to have. Two years later, in August 1956, she gave birth to a fourth child in the hospital in Tatamagouche.

"Why did you give him the name of the baby you lost?" I asked.

"I liked it," was Mary's simple answer. "The baby I lost, his middle name came from one of my mother's brothers so I gave Dwayne the middle name of my older brother: Stewart."

For more than five decades, every time she went to buy groceries, attend a graduation ceremony, see the dentist, or visit the cemetery, Mary drove over the bideau. Every time she called Dwayne by name, she spoke the name of the baby who died.

Which brought me back to the reason for my phone call: how did Dwayne end up with his great-aunt's dog tags?

"After Dwayne was born, Aunt Jean stayed here with me because I had phlebitis in my legs again," Mary explained. "I was in bed for six weeks. She took care of Dwayne and ran the house. When she died in 1974, her sister gave me Aunt Jean's medallions and I thought Dwayne should have them since she took care of him when he was a baby."

When I told my husband about the conversation I'd had with his mother, he said he knew there was a baby before him that died, but the grave marker had no name on it.

"She called him Dwayne Jonathan," I said. "She gave you the first name of the son she lost."

He shrugged, unfazed. For him, the story is about the medallions, as he calls them.

"They are a keepsake because Aunt Jean had looked after me when Mum brought me home from the hospital," he said.

What he doesn't realize is that those medallions represent more than the aunt who was watching over him. Since meeting Dwayne, I'd had this sense of a guardian around him. Hearing his death-defying stories—the car crash that killed his best friend when they were eighteen, the accidents he's had on his snowmobile, and the stroke he survived when he was thirty-nine—convinced me that someone must have been watching over him all these years.

Now I know—we both know—there was: the other fella.

4

The Secrets of a Long and Happy Marriage

───── • •• ─────

When I said yes to a blind date with a Nova Scotia country boy, I had no idea what we would talk about over supper or if we had anything more in common than the friend who had fixed us up. I was a city girl from Ontario, just visiting the east coast for a few weeks in the midst of a few health crises. Back home, my father was living in a nursing home in the later stages of dementia and my mother was about to begin treatment for cancer. I was at our summer home in Pugwash both for a brief respite and to see my friend Diana before she underwent surgery to remove a tumour in her esophagus.

Who says yes to a blind date under those circumstances?

Only a woman who walked into that beloved summer home on the hill overlooking Pugwash Harbour and instantly relaxed. Only a woman who was starting to sense that maybe Nova Scotia was where she belonged after all, where her heart was most happy.

Or perhaps our friend the matchmaker was smarter than anyone gave him credit for because a year after that blind date, I married that Nova Scotia country boy on the front deck of that summer home: we were a match made in east coast heaven.

The following June, as Dwayne and I were enjoying our first year of marriage, we celebrated my new in-laws' sixtieth wedding anniversary. This milestone amazed me, even though my own parents were well past forty years of marriage (my father would pass away shortly before their forty-third anniversary). For me, both couples were examples of contentment, for better and worse, for richer and poorer, in sickness and in health.

A few years later, as our fifth wedding anniversary approached, I started to wonder if there was a secret to creating a long and happy marriage.

The first person I contacted was our original matchmaker, Gary Mundle, who had been married to his wife, Carol, for more than two decades at the time of my call. He told me a good marriage is all about communication: "You have to talk. Every day, every night," Gary told me. "I find most couples who break up didn't know how to talk to each other."

Next, I joined my in-laws on the front porch of the farmhouse where they've lived for most of their married life.

"I kiss Mary in the morning and I kiss her good night," Donn told me.

Then I discovered Dwayne and I had followed in his parents' footsteps: their union was the result of a blind date. They were still in high school when Donn's second cousin fixed them up on a double date, but sixty-four years later, neither of them could remember the movie they saw in Springhill that night. They married two years later, at the ages of nineteen and twenty-one. They had three children, worked hard, and led fulfilling lives that revolved around home, farm, and church.

"Donn's parents were awfully good to us," said Mary, whose in-laws lived across the yard in the house where Donn grew up. "They'd come up and stay with the kids when we wanted to get away for our anniversary."

Married in June, Donn and Mary honeymooned in the Annapolis Valley during the Apple Blossom Festival and returned every year for their anniversary. It was a long-standing tradition that allowed them time away from their responsibilities, time to themselves.

"You just make a point of getting along," Mary told me. "You have to overlook things. And there are a lot of times when you have to hold each other up," she admitted. "The time I remember best was when I lost my baby."

Mary's insight into a long marriage reminded me of the challenge my parents faced when my father was diagnosed with Alzheimer's disease. For the next seven years, my mother's devotion and commitment held him up as the disease altered his mind and behaviour. The struggle of their final years together—common for couples who grow old together—would not eclipse the life they'd shared for more than four decades.

"You have to love the person almost more than you love yourself," my mother told me. "You both have to love each other unselfishly, and you have to laugh. You have to be able to laugh with each other and at each other when things happen." This explains why there was so much laughter in our home when I was growing up.

For me, watching my mother take care of her husband as he disappeared in his early sixties made me aware that whatever time Dwayne and I have together—five years or twenty-five—should not be taken for granted. This is something we are particularly aware of, not only because of our fourteen-year age difference, but also because both our first marriages ended in divorce.

This could be the secret to a long and happy second marriage then: daily gratitude. You wake up every morning next to the person you feel lucky to have met and married, the person with whom you were willing to try marriage again. With whom you wish you were already celebrating twenty-five years of marriage.

An unexpected conversation with my oldest nephew, George, reminded me of why I married Dwayne. One afternoon while I was visiting my sister and her family in Atlanta, George flopped down on the couch next to me and said, "You divorced the first guy you married." It wasn't a question.

You've gotta love sisters.

I told him that was true.

"Didn't you get along?" he asked.

"No," I answered. "We weren't compatible."

Instead of asking what compatible meant, George said, "So you divorced him. Then you found Uncle Dwayne. Did you want him because he is a builder?"

I laughed gently, not wanting him to think it wasn't a good question. It was a great question, actually.

"No, I wanted him because he has a big heart and he cares about people."

"That's good, too," George replied.

And I realized it was. It was very good. If, during your first date, you think, "This guy would drop whatever he was doing if someone called and needed help," that's the guy you want to commit to for better or worse, in sickness and health.

At the time of this conversation, George's parents—my sister, Araminta, and her husband, Jason—had been married fifteen years. When I asked what she thought the secret to a long and happy marriage was, my sister told me the secret is not giving up: "We've had our share of challenges and most people would walk away when things get hard. We've always joked that people with money are the ones who can afford to get divorced." Joking aside, Araminta added, "People need to be honest with each other, and nice. We need more nice in the world."

Just when I thought I'd figured out all the secrets to a long and happy marriage, a few years later my search circled back to my in-laws—the only people I know personally who have been married a long, long time and still love and cherish their time together despite health problems, mobility limitations, and all the other trials that come with ageing bodies paired with strong spirits.

My mother-in-law celebrated her eighty-seventh birthday in the hospital during a two-week rest to try and heal a leg ulcer that had grown into a wide open wound, raw and painful.

"There is so much I should be doing at home," Mary said to me during a morning visit.

"Which is why you are in the hospital, Mary," I replied.

She was in the hospital because her leg ulcer was worsening, to the point that amputation had slipped onto the bottom of the list of possible outcomes, and here she was, still committed to doing everything without help. Committed to doing everything for her husband, just as she'd been doing for more than sixty-seven years of marriage.

Perhaps that, too, is a secret: a clear division of labour, a fixed list of expectations.

Mary worked as hard as her husband, and provided for their family. It was the way of life Mary knew, having grown up in a rural area and married a man who ran a farm, drove truck, and worked in the woods. Of course the house was her domain; she was in it twenty-four hours a day, making three meals, baking bread and pies, cleaning floors, washing clothes, and feeding people.

I have great respect for Mary's work, for her dedication to her family, and as a strong, capable woman. What I am most in awe of is now, at age eighty-seven, with severe arthritis and recurring leg ulcers, with a hernia, for heaven's sake, she continues to see herself as a farm wife whose job is to take care of everyone, particularly—and most stubbornly—her husband.

There was a moment as Mary returned home from the hospital, her leg slowly on the mend, that I saw her life, her devotion, and her care from another perspective. My husband had picked his mother up and brought her home after she was discharged. Donn stood at the open door, leaning heavily on his cane, watching her slow progress from the truck, along the walkway, and up the stairs towards him. I only had a view of his profile but I could see his eyes flush with tears.

"It's good to have you home, dear," he said, his voice shaky with emotion. As she wobbled in the doorway, he leaned forward and kissed her. He was blocking the doorway, she was tired and sick, wanting to be inside and sitting down, but that first kiss, that welcome-home peck mattered to him. It could not wait.

I thought about the few times I went with my husband and his father to visit Mary in the hospital and how Donn always kissed her hello and goodbye. I'd watch him lean over the bed, lean the bulk of his body over his tiny wife shrinking into the mattress of the hospital bed, and worry about him losing his balance and falling on her.

But, like everything else they've insisted on doing for themselves—and for others—for nearly seven decades, he would kiss his wife whenever he could, for as long as he could. I realized it was worth the effort, worth the risk, to kiss the same lips you've kissed since you were twenty. You never know when it could be your last.

"We had a good life," my mother-in-law told me that afternoon a few years ago when we sat on their front porch. From our seats, we overlooked the horse pasture and the original farmhouse where my husband's older brother lives now, the river beyond that. "We've climbed the mountain and now we're heading down the other side."

Holding each other up. Kissing good night and good morning. Being nice and talking about everything. These are the secrets—as well as the blessings and the miracle—of a long and happy marriage.

5

Must Love Dogs

⸺ • •• ⸺

*T*he decision to interview Cathy Duyinsveld for a newspaper column satisfied my very slim criteria: she was a local person doing
something interesting. I'd been told she was a teacher "up north" and
while that might not seem like much to go on, I've learned you just
need one detail, one conversation starter, one opening question to get
the real story, which is often better than you expected.

After I knocked on the old farmhouse door at Cathy's family's farm in Wallace Bay, I smiled at the long, deep toenail scratches
grooved into the wood below the doorknob by generations of farm
dogs. Once Cathy opened the door and invited me in, I noticed her
uneven gait and the patch over her right eye. That's when I recalled
another detail about this woman: five years earlier, she'd been badly
injured in a horseback riding accident. Suddenly, I remembered hearing the news and connecting her name to a local farm family but never
hearing how she'd fared after the mishap.

That couldn't be my opening question, however; that part of the story would come later. First, I wanted to know where she now lived, and why. As we sat at the kitchen table of the house she grew up in, I learned Cathy's career and accident were really part of a bigger, more wonderful story of love at first sight.

The middle of three children, Cathy grew up on the farm but was the only sibling to pursue a non-farming career. After high school, she headed first to Dalhousie University for a bachelor of science in biology, and then to Acadia University for a bachelor of education. After graduating in 1995, Cathy applied for teaching jobs throughout the Maritimes but wasn't hired. This didn't bother her very much since she had gone back to work as a groundskeeper at the local golf course, a job she'd held since high school.

"The superintendent of the golf course told me if teaching didn't work out, I could eventually become a golf superintendent," Cathy remembered. "I was all gung-ho, we were making plans. I loved that job at the golf course because I loved being outside and meeting the golfers."

At the end of summer, Cathy responded to a job posting in the newspaper, this time for a teaching position in remote northeast Quebec. She flew to Montreal for an interview and by the time she'd returned home to Wallace Bay, they'd called to tell her she had the job. A week later, at age twenty-six, Cathy left home. Left the family farm. Left the beloved job at the golf course. Left her friends and family to move to a community near the Quebec–Labrador border, accessible only by plane or ferry from mainland Newfoundland. She left a small, rural area for an even smaller, more remote place.

As she flew to her new community in a small plane with six other passengers, Cathy looked out the window. Raised in lush Cumberland County along the Northumberland Strait, the isolation of her new home shocked her.

"There were no houses, no trees. There was nothing down there but rocks and ponds and moss," she said.

Cathy arrived at the village of St. Pauls River, with a population of less than five hundred English-speaking people, and settled into the one-bedroom apartment provided by the school board.

Within three days, she started working at a school with a total of seventy students from kindergarten to grade eleven. (In Quebec, students move on to the CGEP program, the equivalent of grade twelve in other provinces.)

As Cathy settled in, she met her neighbours in the six-unit apartment building, most of whom were other first-year teachers. Cathy kept her homesickness at bay by throwing herself into work and hanging out with the other teachers on weekends. An active person, she made the most of the barren but beautiful landscape around the village.

"The other teachers were very active and good to do stuff with," Cathy explained. "We went adventuring together. We climbed the hills in the fall and went cross-country skiing on the river in the winter. It was good for a new teacher: you're young, you're starting out. I enjoyed it and made some good friends," she said.

The incentives for living in an isolated fishing village included three paid trips a year, so Cathy used her first trip to go home in October, visit her family, pack up her car, and adopt a puppy. If there was one thing this Wallace Bay farm girl refused to live without, it was a dog.

Shortly before Cathy took the job in St. Pauls River, her childhood dog had died at the age of sixteen. She wouldn't have left Brandy behind, so his death was actually a blessing in disguise: it allowed her to take the job in a remote location without guilt. But it didn't take long in her strange new home for Cathy to begin craving canine companionship. She adopted Sam, an Australian shepherd, during that first trip home and when her parents drove to St. Pauls River with Cathy's car full of dishes and other household items, Sam came with them.

While Cathy went about her new life as a teacher and dog mom, she was unaware that she had caught the eye of Maurice Keats, a good friend of the older English teacher who lived in the apartment next to Cathy. Born and raised in St. Pauls River, Maurice worked as a crab and cod fisher, as well as a salmon fishing guide during the summer.

"Cathy got her dog that fall," Maurice said from the couch in his mother-in-law's living room, "and that's when I realized she loved dogs. I loved dogs, too, so I started walking my mother's dog back and forth in front of her place to see if we could meet that way."

Alas, Maurice was never quite at the right place at the right time. Eventually, the following spring, a mutual friend introduced them at the local bar. For their first date, Cathy invited Maurice to her apartment ostensibly to eat cheesecake but she really wanted to see if he passed the dog test.

"Sam went right over and chewed his bone by Maurice's feet so I knew he couldn't be a bad fellow."

Three years later, in 1999, the couple married at the Wallace Baptist Church. They then returned to St. Pauls River, where both of their daughters were born.

After their second daughter arrived, Cathy and Maurice decided to move back to Nova Scotia, to where Cathy grew up, in order to give their girls more opportunities. Cathy got a job teaching at the high school in Pugwash but quickly and surprisingly discovered she didn't like it.

"Coming from a really small community like St. Pauls River to a class with twenty-plus kids was a whole different thing," she admitted. "They were great students in Pugwash but I missed my ten to fifteen students I knew so well. That's a whole different environment for teaching."

Cathy fulfilled her commitment for one school year in Pugwash, and then the family returned to eastern Quebec.

"You either hate it or you love it," Maurice said.

And Cathy loves it. An avid photographer and cross-country skier, she enjoys the best of both worlds: a job and an active lifestyle in St. Pauls River, and summers at the farm in Wallace Bay. She would make the drive to Nova Scotia in two days, pushing to get home with the girls and their dogs and cats, leaving Maurice behind to spend the summer working at a remote salmon fishing camp forty-two kilometres from St. Pauls River.

"Summer at the farm means I get to be a kid again," Cathy said. "I get to roam around the farm, take photos, help my brother John out. I love the farm and the girls love their ponies."

At the end of the summer of 2009, however, Cathy and the girls did not return to St. Pauls River in time to start school. During a final horse ride with her daughters, Cathy's life changed course again.

"I'm not a great rider," she told me. "The horse stumbled and I fell off."

Even though she was wearing a helmet, Cathy suffered a head injury that affected the right side of her body—her right eye, arm, and leg—but thankfully not her speech.

Maurice, who had to be tracked down at his remote fishing camp, picked up the story at this point, telling the part Cathy doesn't know because she was in a coma.

"We were in Halifax until Christmas," Maurice explained. "We had to rent a place in Halifax while Cathy was in hospital and we got a ton of support from both [Wallace Bay and St. Pauls River]. They held Bingo [nights] back home to raise money for us, and the fishermen I worked with sent thousands of dollars. They were unbelievable. We had a lot of help to get through it."

Once Cathy emerged from her coma, she began the tough work of rehabilitation; bringing mobility back to her leg and arms. She was off work for two years while she recovered, and once she'd battled her way back to good health, she then had to battle a school board who had heard "head injury" and written her off. Between her determination to recover and her husband's gifts of technology to aid her writing in the classroom—"My handwriting is fine but it's slow and not pretty," she says—Cathy proved she was ready and able to return to the science lab full-time in the fall of 2012.

"It felt good to prove them wrong," she smiled. "I call it being stubborn."

Her husband said he never doubted her fighting spirit. We sat in silence for a bit, our conversation winding down, but as I packed up my notebook and digital recorder, Maurice began speaking again.

"The nicest thing she ever said to me was when she came out of her coma," he said. "She didn't really know anybody but she looked at me and said, 'I haven't got a clue who you are but I know I love you.'"

His words hung in the warm, dusty air of the farmhouse. Was everyone else swallowing as hard as I was? After a sixteen-year marriage, two daughters, and several dogs, Cathy and Maurice could finally say it was love at first sight.

6

My Husband Knows Jack About Decorating

———·••——

After I'd moved home from Vancouver into my parents' town-house in Ontario, I asked my mother if I could redecorate her guest room. It was clear my first marriage could not be saved and both parents needed me to stay and help care for my father, who had Alzheimer's disease. The changes were superficial—paint and a bedspread—but I felt it was important to make the space my own.

This idea came from a magazine article that recommended re-decorating after a breakup to remove all memories of the person who was no longer living in the space. Granted, I was in a new home, but I still felt justified in wanting to make this bedroom feel like my own; fresh paint, new bedding, my choice of art on the walls, and my desk made the space feel new, but also familiar.

I didn't feel the same way when I moved into the old house on Pugwash Point Road my parents had bought and fixed up while I lived in Vancouver. To me, the "maid's quarters" upstairs were perfect; they had a distinctive charm thanks to the sharply sloped ceilings, which were wooden and painted the same bright blue as the floors. When I added something of my own, it was a piece of sea glass, a sand dollar, or a heart-shaped rock from the beach at the end of the road.

A few years later, I met my Nova Scotia country boy. After stepping through the knee-high weeds growing through the cracks of the paving bricks at his front door, I realized it wasn't only the man who needed refurbishing; the house required some TLC as well. Dwayne introduced me to his country life by taking me over Economy Mountain on a four-wheeler and down the River Philip in a canoe, but he also allowed me to show him the potential in his then-twenty-eight-year-old house…which is a nice way of saying he caved to my redecorating suggestions.

When he first built his home in 1979, Dwayne planted trees all around the yard: pine, spruce, maple, and birch. Right in front of the house grew a mature Manitoba maple, a grey birch, and two full-grown lilac trees. He had curtains swathing all the front windows, though, and the verdant front yard was hardly noticeable from indoors.

"You know," I said one evening while we sat at the dining room table after supper, "a patio door here in the dining room and a deck out front there would be really nice."

I was just visiting from Ontario for Thanksgiving weekend but I couldn't help myself. I remembered that article about making a space your own after a breakup, and here was Dwayne's home looking exactly like it did when his first wife lived there. I could see so much potential in the home—it was time to be free from the tyranny of the wallpaper border.

I'd been back in Ontario for a few weeks when Dwayne left a message on my parents' answering machine: "It turns out there are four layers of border in the dining room," he growled. "There's so much steam coming out of my ears, I'm surprised it's not falling off the wall."

Yet when I arrived for another visit after the holidays, he happily wrote down the coordinating paint codes I gave him. Months later, I was delighted to see "Spun Toffee" on the living room walls and "Cinnamon Sizzle" in the dining room. Not a flowered border in sight.

Living in a house is much different than visiting it, however, and once I moved into Dwayne's home a few months before our wedding, I realized I'd faced the least of the decorating challenges. I could no longer pretend there wasn't a huge cedar gun cabinet taking up one entire corner of the dining room.

Everything about the home, right down to the plastic totes and cardboard boxes in the basement, recalled the past. By this time, I'd read a magazine article about neuroplasticity; the idea that "neurons that fire together wire together." In Dwayne's context, this meant every time he walked into his house and saw the same colours, layout, furniture, and curtains chosen by his former wife, the neurons associated with her and their marriage fired up.

By the time our wedding rolled around at the end of July, every room was refreshed. There were use-up-all-the-leftover-paint stripes on one wall of the sunroom, a new shelving unit in the kitchen for our dishes, and a new deck out front which we used every day.

While it may seem obnoxious to take over a man's house so completely, part of the reason we were instantly compatible was because we both wanted to find a heart and a home to call our own. This is what we did that spring: we gardened and redecorated. We did it together and it made us happy; it came naturally. I picked the paint and Dwayne brought it home. When he returned from work in the evening, some room in the house looked different.

When it came to the bedroom, it wasn't feng shui that guided our decisions—it was neuroplasticity. It was the final project because it took more time to get a feel for what we needed.

"It's all field and woods out back here," I said one day, standing at the shoulder-high window. "It's a shame we can't see the view when we're lying in bed."

The next thing I knew, Dwayne had measured and installed two windows that almost reached floor to ceiling. The walls went from pale taupe to "Blue Lagoon," and the dirty grey carpet transformed one evening into a dark laminate floor. The new bedspread and pillow shams—"What's a sham?" Dwayne had to ask—coordinated perfectly. It wasn't only traces of a former life that had to go; I refused to sleep another night under moose antlers, family heirloom or not.

Back in 1893, when he was working in the woods in the Miramichi, Dwayne's great-grandfather, Samuel Mattinson, shot the moose wearing the six-point rack. As quintessentially country as antlers are, they were far too large—and unsettling—to have hanging over the bed. It would have been a shame if the antlers had been a deal-breaker, but thankfully Dwayne didn't mind putting the antlers in the basement.

And so, when we fell into bed in the wee hours of our wedding night, we were in the space we'd created, where we would forge neural pathways of peace and happiness and marital bliss. His house was my house. My stuff was his stuff. Our newlywed neurons were now firing and wiring together.

My father died shortly before our second wedding anniversary, and my mother decided to sell her home in Ontario and split her time between Pugwash Point and Georgia, where her grandchildren lived. One afternoon a moving van backed into our lane and deposited my share of stuff from my parents' house, most notably their king-sized bed, antique dressers, and the Robert Bateman paintings my father had collected.

"We're going to need more walls," my husband commented.

Eventually, my mother sold the house on Pugwash Point too, "because it's not the same without your father there." Dwayne and I agreed to build a large addition on our home so she could live with us.

Actually, the agreement went more like this: "Mum, if you give me a new kitchen, you can move in with us."

As always, Dwayne listened to our ideas, vetoed the ones that made no sense or could not be done—"Sorry, Lynda," he told my mother, "we can't build you a tower"—and hired the crew for the next, even bigger renovation.

So imagine my surprise when my agreeable, deferring-to-my-impeccable-tastes husband returned home late one day with his own contribution. He'd gone to Dartmouth for an appointment and his friend Al went with him. I should have known that a road trip with Al would involve a detour to the outdoor store near Elmsdale.

"By the way, I picked us up a new pet today," he said, innocently enough, after he'd been home for a bit.

"Okay…" I said, unsure why he was grinning like that.

He'd made it clear on many occasions that two cats and two dogs inside the house and a dozen chickens and two rabbits outside was sufficient. I didn't think he'd brought home a donkey or a goat or any other animal I really wanted, so I figured the "pet" would be a giant concrete rooster for the garden.

"It's out in the truck," he said and went to fetch it.

I was sitting at the dining room table checking email on the laptop when he returned. When I looked up, an enormous black bear with a huge pink tongue and giant white teeth was roaring at me.

"Holy crap!" I screamed and leaped out of my chair, putting distance between me and the (very realistic) bear. Except that my husband was holding it in his arms because it had no body—it was just a bear head.

"What were you thinking? What did you do?" I hollered, because when your husband goes to the city to see his surgeon and returns with a mounted bear head, something has obviously happened.

"We stopped at Hnatiuk's Fishing and Hunting Store on the way down and someone had brought in a bear, put a down payment on getting the head mounted, but never came back for it," Dwayne explained. "So I traded a gun for it."

Of course he did. It's what any self-respecting Nova Scotia country boy would do: trade a gun for a mounted bear head.

"Oh, and his name is Jack. Where do you want me to hang him?"

"You can't hang that thing in the house!" I squawked. "The dogs haven't even blinked since you brought it inside. And how long do you think it will take the kitten to discover he can hang off the lower jaw?"

"You really don't want Jack in the house?"

By then, I couldn't tell if Dwayne was serious or not but I looked behind me at the wide fireplace mantel where I'd placed three oil lamps, an ironwood sculpture of a coyote from California, and the eagle painting my father had loved. Dwayne had never complained about my knick-knacks, never objected to every flat surface being covered in either picture frames or books, never balked at a colour, never even questioned the green kitchen cupboards.

But hang Jack in the living room? Have that mouth roaring at me every morning as I did yoga or in the evenings when we watched TV?

"Jack can live in the new garage with the moose antlers," I said. As Dwayne carried his new pet out of the house, he muttered, "If you write about this, I get to bring Jack back in the house and hang him above the fireplace."

7

Hobgoblins

When I was a kid in the 1970s, we lived above my father's business—a funeral home—so we could never make a big deal out of Halloween. There were no skeletons hanging on our doors or jack-o'-lanterns grinning from our doorstep—not even at the private entrance around back. The upside to this was both parents could take my sister and me trick-or-treating since no one had to remain home and answer the door. We wandered up Buck Street behind the funeral home, then across Division Street to the neighbourhood around the church. Once we were done visiting our friends' homes in town, we drove to the countryside where our grandparents and a few other relatives lived.

When I think of Halloween, this drive to the country to visit Grandma and Grandpa Jewell, Gramma and Grampa George, and Aunt Reta is what first comes to mind. We stopped at their homes for long visits and my mother took a couple of photographs of my sister and me dressed as Santa Claus, or a princess, or Miss Canada, standing next to the chair our relative sat in. The visits and the photographs created far more important treasures than the candy in our pillowcases.

Outside of that drive to the country, my experience with trick-or-treating was typical: happily tromping around suburban sidewalks, going from house to closely spaced house. In the country, however, there are great distances between homes and not nearly as many.

I've often wondered why my husband insists on carving jack-o'-lanterns for our steps and makes sure all the outside lights are on after supper on the thirty-first. There are only ever a few neighbourhood kids who show up, and we don't have children of our own. Yet every year, my husband brings home small bags of chips and mini chocolate bars. I've sensed there's more to it than getting to eat the leftovers.

"What was Halloween like when you were a kid?" I finally asked after a few years of watching his annual ritual.

"Exciting," he said without hesitation. "Really exciting."

"Really? Did you go trick-or-treating?"

"Of course."

By the time he finished telling me about Halloween in the country in the 1960s, I was in love with him all over again.

Dwayne and his siblings grew up in the river valley halfway between Oxford and Port Howe; the hamlet known as "Riverview" boasted several farming families and a church, although the school Dwayne's father attended in the 1930s was long gone, the sign from the old school now hanging in his machine shed.

On Halloween night, a bunch of the neighbourhood kids went out together, about seven or eight of them. The four Casey kids and Ronnie McLellan arrived at Dwayne's house and from there, the band of beggars—friends and siblings—set off down the gravel road. They went parent-free and called at a dozen homes during their five-kilometre walk to Port Howe.

"Dad would pick us up when he was finished doing chores," Dwayne explained, "so we left a pile of stones on the road in front of every house we visited."

The image of a group of kids walking and chattering along an unpaved road, yelling "trick or treat!" at each house they stopped at, then pausing to scoop dirt and stones into a pile so Dwayne's father could track them down delighted me.

"The farthest we ever made it was Bert and Flossie Bowser's house just before the bridge," my husband said.

What a huge distance for a group of children to walk in the dark, yet they thought nothing of it. Dwayne's dad would pick them up and take them around Port Howe, back then a cluster of fourteen houses and a general store, for a final round of candy rustling.

"I remember walking in snow flurries some years," Dwayne said.

My friend Jane, three years younger than Dwayne, was born and raised in Oxford Junction, which is also along the River Philip but way upriver, where it is no longer tidal water. Her memories, too, are of a band of eight kids heading out on their (paved) road, Route 321 south of Oxford. A tantalizingly empty church and cemetery lay en route to their final destination of Newt and June Rector's house.

"We would always get into that cemetery and raise hell because nobody was afraid of what was in there," Jane told me with a big grin. "We knew we could get in the back entry of the church and there was an old church bell in a wooden crate in there. So we'd get in and pull the clapper and ring the bell. Nobody did that unless it was Halloween."

That doesn't sound so bad, I thought.

"There were apple trees back there, too, and by that time, all the apples had fallen so we would hide behind the headstones and throw apples at the cars."

Jane assured me that was the worst they did—until she remembered they'd also hide behind headstones and jump out to scare "the livin' daylights" out of little kids.

"Once in a while you'd get your hands on an old sheet and go walking around in the cemetery like a ghost. That was pretty fun."

It appears that old sheet was as good as any costume in Oxford Junction. In those days, especially in the country, a store-bought costume was rare. In fact, Jane never had one.

"Sometimes I'd have a mask but mostly a costume was whatever old clothes we could find around the house, like old dresses and Dad's work socks," she said. "We were never anything in particular, you know, the boys were never Superman or Spiderman; it was just whatever we could find and whatever makeup we could plaster on our faces."

It was the same for Dwayne and his crowd. When I asked him what costumes he wore as a kid, he said they were just cast-off clothes scrounged from the chests upstairs at his grandparents' house.

"We went up to Granny's kitchen chamber and put on whatever old clothes we could find. We used to wear the old jackets and scarves and hats. Most of them were ten times too big for us." They solved the size problem by stuffing the clothes with hay. "We used lipstick to change our faces and some kids wore masks," he added. "One year, I had a Lone Ranger mask so I wore my cowboy hat and my holster with my cap guns." He laughed a nostalgic, happy laugh.

Dwayne and Jane's memories stir up my own, long tucked away once I stopped dressing up. They had me thinking how my mother did Halloween: homemade costumes, themed tablecloth, and a few simple decorations (specifically the happy old crone: five feet tall with striped stockings, a huge, green, warty nose, and a cauldron full of cheerful mice. She hung on our dining room wall one day a year).

Just as Dwayne raided his grandmother's clothes chest, I headed to my mother's closest for inspiration. The gown for my princess costume was the red caftan my father had given her for Christmas one year. When my sister went as Santa Claus, she wore her own almost-outgrown red pyjamas and a mask made from a paper plate with cotton balls glued to it.

I see your hay stuffing and raise you one cotton-ball beard.

Nothing could top my mother's old fox-fur coat—we tried to incorporate it into our costumes every year—or the tangled, long-haired wig the beauty salon next door had "gifted" us for dress-up. I wore the wig to my sixth birthday party before it became part of my witch costume six months later.

Although our experiences were vastly different—mine in town, his in the country; mine in the seventies, his in the sixties—we both share memories of a Halloween that was simple and homemade, not a commercial holiday.

Now I understand my husband's insistence on giving out Halloween candy: he wants to be part of creating memories for a new generation. But as I listen to his stories about cobbling together a costume and Jane's stories about pranks, I have to admit the Halloween of today can't hold a candle to the simple, homemade, innocent Halloweens of years gone by.

When I consider how many perfect and identical Queen Elsas, Maleficents, Spidermen, and Ninja Turtles wander the streets on October 31, it makes me nostalgic. I miss when a band of beggars wearing straw-stuffed old clothes would head out for a long walk on a gravel road to collect apples, molasses kisses, and peanuts, thinking it was the most exciting night of the year.

8

Nanny and Grampie get an iPad

——— · ·· ———

My in-laws are of the post-First World War generation that believes you don't replace things, you fix them. If the couch starts
to sag in the middle, you place a board underneath for support. If the
television breaks, you load it onto the truck—all seventy-five pounds
of cabinet and picture tube—to get it repaired. You do not buy a flat-
screen television because the large, wooden cabinet is an essential
piece of furniture; what would the picture frames and knick-knacks
sit on?

I have to say this is the great divide when it comes to the way my
husband and I each grew up: I in urban Ontario, he in rural Nova
Scotia. By the time I was eighteen I'd lived in three different towns

and five different houses; he lived in the same house for twenty-one years before building his own. When you move, a culling happens: worn-out furniture doesn't make the trip to the freshly renovated new house, books you'll never read again get donated, and broken trinkets get thrown out regardless of their sentimental value. My parents were not "fix it" types, and my father was not a farmer.

Not being raised on a farm, I knew nothing of broken machinery, spare parts, junk that "might come in handy some day," and the challenge of not living five minutes from a Canadian Tire. So when I discovered, a year or so into my new country life, that my husband's then-eighty-year-old mother dragged a portable washing machine from the porch to the kitchen sink to do her laundry, I told him, "We are buying your mother a new washing machine."

For months after, my mother-in-law called every Monday afternoon. "I used your washing machine today, Sara," she'd say. I always had the impression she wondered why we'd wasted our money on a new machine when her ten-year-old one was in perfectly good shape.

There is a strong resistance to change in rural Nova Scotia, an attitude that is both admirable and unfortunate. Is it one of the main differences between city people and country people? Or it is a specifically Maritime phenomenon? I think it's a 30-70 split, but don't ask me to back that up with any scientific data. I'm a city girl who moved around a lot. For me, change is the norm—perhaps even a craving—not a bitter pill to swallow.

Then again, perhaps it's not resistance to change so much as it's pure stubbornness: that intractable "this is the way we've always done it" attitude people who have lived in the same place their entire lives seem to be born with. The rural inheritance, if you will.

I would be remiss, however, if I didn't confess to my own pièce de résistance, my own stubborn refusal to do what everyone is doing: I don't use a smart phone. We don't need the added expense, and I work from home and sit at a computer most of the day. I spend far too much time perusing Facebook and Twitter as it is—it's nice to get a break from all that when I leave the house.

When I lived in Vancouver, I never understood my fellow dog walkers who could wander through lovely, tree-lined streets without paying any attention to their dogs or noticing the cherry blossoms for yakking away on their phones. In rural Nova Scotia, when I walk through the woods or on the beach, I want to be listening to the birds in the trees or collecting sea glass and shells, not looking at a screen. Maybe I can understand a bit of my mother-in-law's stubbornness because part of me is proud of my resistance to the electronic zombification of human beings.

So when my husband informed me my in-laws were getting an iPad for Christmas from the grandsons who don't live nearby, I was stunned into silence. Then I started to laugh.

"What a waste of money!" I cried. "What on earth would they need an iPad for?"

"Apparently, they'll be able to see their great-grandchildren and talk to them," Dwayne explained.

That shut me up. My nieces and nephews live in Georgia and seeing them on Skype is far better than talking on the phone.

In late January my dog, Stella, and I walked down to my in-laws' house for a visit. As soon as I sat down in their living room, I asked a question that would alter the course of my entire afternoon.

"Did you ever get your internet hooked up?" I asked.

"Oh, yes," Mary answered. "Here, I'll just put the kettle on while you show us how this works."

This was the iPad my mother-in-law had thrust into my hands. In their late eighties, Mary and Donn refused to even leave a message on a telephone answering machine ("I won't talk to no machine," Donn said when we first started using them). What on earth would they do with a "thingamajiggy" like an iPad?

Obviously, there had been some tricks employed to get Mary and Donn to use a new piece of technology: 1) buy it and install it for them, and 2) promise them more face time with their newest great-grandchildren.

Someone had already set up an email account for the iPad, the first step to using the FaceTime app. My in-laws were itching to learn how it worked. Forget going slowly so Mary and Donn could understand my instructions; I had to go slowly to process my in-laws having an iPad and being excited about it.

Or rather, Mary was excited: it quickly became apparent Donn preferred his face time with the window overlooking the road.

"You have an email from Beverley," I said to Mary. I wrote her daughter back to tell her that the email was working but I had been commandeered to get FaceTime running. I told her Mary had said she was going to boil water for tea, but the way she continued to look over my shoulder suggested a cuppa anytime soon was unlikely.

My broad hint was lost, though, because at that moment the iPad rang. Two buttons appeared on the screen, and I held it up to show Mary I was tapping "Accept." Her grandson, Peter, appeared on the screen and Mary's face was in a small box in the corner.

It worked! Nanny and Grampie could FaceTime.

After her brief call with Peter, Mary seemed rather excited by the iPad. She disappeared for a few minutes to finally put the kettle on (understanding that one must keep the hostage hydrated) but was soon back at my shoulder asking questions. She wasn't joking around or dismissing it as "too hard to understand" like my own mother; Mary was taking this seriously, eager to understand.

My mother-in-law is a woman who likes to be connected—especially to family—and values information. Over sixty-five years, she has watched her community shrink to a few long-time residents, church attendance dwindle to a few dedicated members, and her grandchildren and great-grandchildren experience things she never did growing up in the 1930s and '40s. There are names in the newspaper she doesn't recognize and the children of children she once knew are moving away.

From her family she hears words like "email, internet, Facebook" described as tools for gathering and sharing information, so she wants to understand, even use these tools, if this is the way to stay in the loop. The finger that reached out to tap the mail icon may have been gnarled with arthritis, but Mary's mind was in very good shape. Everything was set up, so, thinking I might get some tea and be allowed to leave, I toured her around the main display.

"Tap that icon for email."

Nanny and Grampie had an email account!

"Tap that icon for FaceTime."

Nanny and Grampie were going to chat with people using a computer!

As I snuck one of Donn's gumdrops for an energy boost, I heard Mary dial the phone.

"I just want to let you know Sara is fine," she told my husband. "She's helping us with the iPad."

"Help! Help!" I hollered but Mary just chuckled as she hung up.

By this time, it was ticking on to four o'clock. If I stayed any longer, I was going to need to eat a meal here. Mary may have been embracing new technology but she'd still try to feed me, emptying the contents of the refrigerator onto the table like I'd spent the afternoon stacking wood instead of tapping a screen.

The time to escape was now. Luckily, Donn had recently undergone a cataract operation and Mary wasn't as swift on her feet as she used to be (although both were armed with canes which could be used to trip me), so in a moment when they were distracted, I broke out of my chair, dashed through the kitchen, grabbed my coat and the dog's leash, and ran out the door, hollering at Stella to keep up; I was slipping and sliding on the ice and snow but oh, so grateful to be free.

All teasing aside, I was impressed with Mary's willingness to accept this new gadget, considering she won't get a flat-screen television because she can't display framed photos of her great-grandchildren on top of it. While stubbornness may be at the root of her resistance to change, I admire the flip side of the coin: the determination and persistence that fuels her eagerness to learn something new for the sake of her family.

9

The Artist's Way

A few years ago, Jennifer Houghtaling's booth at the Pugwash Farmers' Market was a riotous offering of richly coloured mugs and bowls, homemade granola and honey, several varieties of bread, and hand-knitted toques, but there was no sign of her other weaving. As I purchased my cranberry-bran loaf, I told her I wanted to buy one of her alpaca wool blankets as a Christmas gift. "Oh, I've got to get back to that," she responded. "I haven't done any weaving since February."

Unfortunately for me, Jenn never did return to weaving. Now thirty-five, Jenn is a wife and mother of two school-age children—and she knows creativity happens in cycles and shifts with age. Whether she is juggling four or five projects or is immersed in one intensive task, she has an admirable work ethic but she also follows her passion. That passion has taken her from British Columbia to Fredericton, Vancouver, and Thailand, ultimately ending—of all places—in Pugwash.

Our backgrounds couldn't be more different, yet our journeys are similar: young women trying to find their place in the world and ultimately discovering it on the red soil of rural Nova Scotia. In this, I feel a kinship with Jenn. I also have a deep admiration for her devotion to her artistic energy and an appreciation for her journey of self-discovery and how it lead her to creativity, love, and family on the east coast.

Born and raised on a four-hundred-acre ranch near Prince George, British Columbia, Jenn was driving a tractor by the age of ten, and helping her father tend to cows, horses, sheep, and pigs. Because the ranch was remote, Jenn was homeschooled until she was ten years old. Her education covered the basics, including the kind of home economics you don't get in school.

"My grandmother lived a kilometre away from us until I was fourteen, and we baked almost every day," Jenn said. "She and my mom also taught me to crochet and knit."

After graduating from high school, Jenn enrolled in university to study nursing. She'd been taught, both at home and at school, that what mattered most were a degree and a good job. She only completed one semester.

"I chose nursing because I wanted to help people while I was making money to pay my bills, but the first semester was all theory. I can't learn like that," she told me. "I learn through hands-on, by someone helping me do something. If I'd been in a hospital with nurses showing me what to do, I'd probably be a nurse now."

By the time she was twenty-one, Jenn was serving tables and working in a convenience store. The day her boss at the store told her she'd soon be the supervisor, Jenn quit. A friend suggested she try tree planting to get away from home (and other people's expectations), so she hired on with a company and began planting trees all over British Columbia and Alberta.

After a few years, she got involved with a fellow tree-planter and musician named Ben, and when he moved to Fredericton, she followed. Even though they broke up within a month of her arrival, she discovered something she didn't even know she'd been searching for: the New Brunswick College of Craft and Design.

"It blew my mind," she said. "I didn't know there was a place where they taught you to be an artist."

Jenn enrolled at the college in Fredericton, intending to learn weaving and textiles, but since she also had to take a third course, she chose pottery.

"I fell in love with that," she remembered. "I'd be in the studio until four o'clock in the morning, just in heaven."

Even there, however, the pressure of expectations dogged her. She wanted to create drums, but her instructors insisted she stick with mugs and bowls. So instead of paying for her final year of school, she bought herself a ticket to Thailand.

"I went by myself because I wanted to know if I could go somewhere far away from everybody I knew, be by myself, and be okay. I wanted to be able to trust the world, to put myself out there and not get hurt," explained Jenn. "There was this meditation centre where you could go and give a donation for a ten-day silent meditation. As soon as I finished it, I swore I would go back at least once a year but I never have."

When her money ran out, Jenn returned to British Columbia where she reunited with Ben and the two went back to planting trees. Despite carefully saving their paycheques, they simply couldn't afford a house in Vancouver. At the same time, Jenn discovered she was pregnant.

"That's when we decided to move to the east coast," she remembered.

Ben is originally from Amherst so when they arrived in February 2007 with their four-month-old son, the couple lived with Ben's mother until the house they bought just outside the village of Pugwash had been fixed up. All of a sudden, they were homeowners who needed to provide for a child. Ben and Jenn's deeply ingrained work ethics helped them find a variety of jobs around the village. With almost five acres of land on Crowley Road, Ben built a market garden and a fifteen-metre greenhouse. Each week, Jenn set up a table at the Pugwash Farmers' Market to sell their produce and her pottery. Despite the baby and the cross-country move, she hadn't given it up.

"I knew I was going to do pottery because I had dragged the contents of my entire studio here," she said.

As demand for Jenn's pottery grew, the couple constructed a two-storey pottery studio out of straw bales and clay just steps from their house. With the help of friends, the studio was completed in a couple of years.

"To have all that space for pottery is just wonderful," Jenn smiled. "Before that, I was crammed in our basement, and in the winter it was so cold down there I'd have to wear my winter coat to keep warm. With pottery, you're putting your hands in water all the time so moving into the studio is really nice," she said. "The temperature in there is perfect. Since the walls are so thick, it's cool in summer and warm in winter."

The routine engrained from her childhood on the ranch to her summers planting trees continues to guide her now: she has a flourishing pottery studio, two bright, wild-haired children, and a husband who has found his creative outlet as a successful landscaper.

"My life has always been about working very hard in the summer and doing nothing all winter," she laughed. These days, though, Jenn does most of her pottery in the wintertime, spending about four hours a day at it, which is easier now that both children are in school.

In a way, Jenn's creative process allows her to travel back to that Thai meditation centre without having to leave Crowley Road. Transforming a lump of clay forces her to focus and becomes a form of meditation; Jenn believes the clay needs a person to tell it what to do.

"If I sit down at the wheel and my mind is doing something else, nothing I make is going to work. If I'm really off somewhere else and I sit down and go through two pots, which have to be tossed away because they don't work, then I get with it and start paying attention," she said. "That focus slows my mind down and sets everything straight. I feel like that for the rest of the day. It's with me all the time, as if I'd actually sat down and meditated."

Originally, her loom sat upstairs in the studio and she had every intention of taking up weaving again. But she found every time she approached the stairs, the pottery wheel lured her away. Eventually, she sold the loom and Ben's musical instruments now fill the space upstairs.

"Our [various] businesses have grown and taken over everything," Jenn admitted. "At first, we had to do everything in order to get known in the community and pay the bills. When one of those businesses takes off, everything else gets dropped."

She now knits, bakes, and cooks for family, gifts, or just for herself. The gardens are for personal use only, not the market. She misses weaving but believes it was time to simplify. She wrote up a list of priorities and while weaving blankets didn't make the list, teaching art to children at the local elementary school did. She even began making drums.

Yet there is still a hint of that young woman who didn't like to be told what to do. Now that she is applying to submit her pottery to juried shows and art galleries, she feels a familiar twinge of expectation, of being told, "You're supposed to do this next."

To deal with that, she pushes the limits, by experimenting with new glaze colours every year. Those glaze colours have become the signature of her "Earth and Vine" designs—deep blue, brown, turquoise, periwinkle, purple. Earth and vine imagery appear in the swirls in the bottom of a serving dish, in the shape of a mug handle, in the patterns she draws around the bottom of a cup. No shape is the same and that's intentional: making pieces exactly the same is simply not her style, although it does make custom orders for matching sets challenging.

A fixture for many years at the Pugwash Farmers' Market, Jenn's products have evolved as she slowly explored and refined her interests, her style, and herself. The support of the community and the friends she has made are as meaningful to her as are her husband, children, and creative pursuits.

"I had no real family here so I wanted to build a family: I wanted people who were close to me, people who would come to my house and feel comfortable and hang out with me. A lot of my close friends are really inspiring and talking with them makes me see what is possible," explained Jenn, who is a member of the Pugwash Artists' Collective. "I need social connections and I'm terrible with those over the phone or internet. I like sitting with people. I love the market and chatting with people all day."

Like me, it took Jenn a while to discover her inner compass but once she did, it seemed to point due east. She followed her heart into the unknown only to discover talents and ambitions she hadn't yet tapped. It appears Jennifer's winding road of self-discovery has culminated in a life reminiscent of the place she began. She may not live on a ranch, her children may not be driving a tractor and helping herd cattle and sheep, but she reached into the earth to see what it could give her and once she was planted, she blossomed.

"I feel rooted now," she says. "We have a good, solid foundation. We have no intention of moving anywhere."

10

The Journey of Granny's Chest

⸺ ⋯ ⸺

Whenever I raise the idea of moving to Mexico, or the coast of Spain, or an island in Greece—usually after a blizzard has knocked out our power for three days—my husband looks at me like I've asked for a divorce. Or another cat.

It is inconceivable to him that we would live anywhere but on these seventy-two acres along the River Philip in northwestern Nova Scotia. Not even a photo of white sand and blue sea can make him say, "Maybe someday." My husband lives where he was born and raised and he will be buried, or scattered, right here in this river valley in Cumberland County. I, on the other hand, flung myself out of the nest when I was eighteen and, despite several returns for re-launching, was quite happy moving around.

What we *do* have in common—genealogically speaking—is a strong family narrative that has informed our idea of time, place, and where we fit into this world. For Dwayne, it was his father's history; for me, it was my mother's.

Dwayne grew up knowing his great-grandfather, Samuel Mattinson, lived in Mount Pleasant, and that Sam's son, Floyd, purchased a property in the river valley when he was a grown man. The big move in the Mattinson family happened almost one hundred years ago when Dwayne's grandparents, Floyd and Margaret, moved the eleven kilometres from Mount Pleasant to the property along the river.

I grew up knowing my great-great-grandparents emigrated from Scotland, England, and Ireland. My British ancestors settled in Toronto and opened a grocery store that my mother's father eventually owned and operated. I wasn't really interested in knowing more until recently, when I came across some surprising information that linked those ancestors with Nova Scotia.

My sister and I grew up with a large, heavy, brown chest in the family room of whatever house we lived in; a box my mother called "Granny's chest." Handcrafted from English oak, it didn't feature ornate carvings, but it did have panels and mouldings with wide wrought-iron handles on each end and a large key-shaped lock on the front. Even when empty, it weighed a ton. We played in it, stored toys and games in it, climbed on it, and napped on it. Wherever we lived, Granny's chest was with us. I never thought of Granny's chest as more than just a place to store stuff, but it is a piece of history that reveals Nova Scotia's role in my ancestors' arrival in Canada.

Two years after my father died, my mother decided to sell the summer house they'd owned on Pugwash Point. Dwayne and I renovated and added on to our home so Mum could live with us. Granny's chest moved in as well, placed beneath one of the windows in her room and covered in an afghan because the cat was keeping up the tradition of napping on it.

One afternoon, I was in my mother's room discussing the details of her family in the context of being a "come-from-away," when my mother casually mentioned Granny's chest came over with her ancestors from England.

"You can still see the paint on the lid of the chest from when they came over," she said.

We went to the chest and pulled off the afghan and I saw it immediately: faded gold paint scrawled on four of the six indented panels. In forty-five years, I had never noticed it.

"Mother, you let us play on this!" I said. There is history—family history and Canadian history—painted on this chest and it wasn't preserved.

"It was always on there, it's just the way the chest was," she said. "Originally, it was the natural wood colour and when I put a clear stain on it in 1972, it came out that dark brown colour." It was that stain kept the paint from wearing off completely.

Enough gold paint remains so "Nova Scotia" is obvious across the bottom left panels, while it looks like "Liverpool" is written across the top left panels. Liverpool to Nova Scotia: the first journey of Granny's chest.

I grilled my mother in a way I'd never grilled her before: Where did Granny's chest come from? Who was Granny? Who did she marry? Where did they come from? All of a sudden, I wanted to know more about my mother's paternal great-grandmother.

"Granny's chest was in the attic at 8 Linden Avenue in Scarborough Junction," my mother said. "That's where my Gran lived. She was married to Henry Everest, my father's father, and Granny was his mother. They would have come through Pier 21 in Halifax." Nova Scotia to Toronto: the second journey of Granny's chest.

Family trees are so complicated! I had to work it out for myself.

"So the Granny of Granny's chest was married to John Everest, your great-grandfather. They immigrated to Canada from England. So the chest could have belonged to your great-grandparents. The chest could have ended up in your Gran's house because she was married to Granny's son."

At that point, I had to sit down. I don't know why, but this was taking my breath away. These were names I'd heard throughout my life, but simply couldn't commit to memory. Now for some reason, this writing on Granny's chest, this connection to the east coast, my family as original "come-from-aways" who landed in Halifax, suddenly took on great significance. When you are born and raised in Canada, just as your parents, grandparents, and great-grandparents were, you don't think you have a connection with immigration. You believe your family has always lived here. You don't think you have an immigrant story. You don't think you have any connection to Pier 21.

Until you do.

Suddenly, Halifax and Nova Scotia are part of my family history. Toronto to Nova Scotia: the third journey of Granny's chest.

This required a research trip to Pier 21 on the waterfront in Halifax. My mother and I weren't in the Family History Room long when we learned—with the help of a staff person named Jason—that Canada didn't start keeping immigration records until 1865. There would be no record of my mother's great-grandparents, who, according to the 1871 census, likely arrived in the 1860s, nor would there be any record of them coming through Pier 21 because it didn't open until 1928.

"They would have come through Pier 2," Jason said, handing me a bundle of stapled papers titled *Remember Pier 2: Halifax's Other Immigrant Gateway.* Pier 2 welcomed almost three million immigrants in the 1860s and underwent an expansion in 1915. It took a beating in the Halifax Explosion of 1917 but its new concrete walls held up and Pier 2 remained open until shortly after Pier 21 opened.

Since there were no immigration records available prior to 1865, my quest for a written record—the name of an ancestor who was processed in Halifax—came to an end. And yet, I do have a written record of sorts: the distinct "Nova Scotia" painted in gold on an old, old chest.

The fact remained that my mother's family—on both the paternal and maternal sides—were immigrants, so my mother and I set off for the Canadian Immigration Hall at Pier 21 to learn about what they might have experienced. Immediately after walking through the glass doors, a large display to the right cycles through black and white photographs of people arriving in Halifax. The moment we arrived, the photo on display was of a group of men with a few children. One man had a toddler in his arms, and a couple of men had cotton bags slung over their shoulders; I can only assume the bags held all their worldly possessions. The group looked ragged, a little unkempt (perhaps even dirty), and definitely tired.

Suddenly, I felt a strong emotional connection to the photo.

Tears filled my eyes as I realized my own ancestors likely looked just like that when they finally stepped off the ship after their voyage. How glad they must have been to arrive, to be on solid ground again after nearly two weeks on the Atlantic Ocean.

The emotion followed me as we walked further into the hall: a large, black-and-white image of a woman holding a young boy hung beside displays posing impossible questions like, "What do you bring?" and "What (or who) do you leave behind?"

Thanks to Jason's assistance in the Family History Room, we knew my mother's great-grandfather, Isaac Latham, whose daughter became my mother's Gran, was born in Ireland and was not married when he arrived in Toronto. We also knew the date his first child was born, so we deduced that he must have left Ireland during the Great Potato Famine of 1846, when he would've been in his mid-twenties.

He could have been one of those men with all his possessions stuffed into a pillowcase slung over one shoulder. But without records, we don't know if he travelled with family or alone. We don't know if he came with a chest full of belongings or only what was in his pockets. What did he bring? Who did he leave behind?

I'm not trying to make Granny's chest out to be some kind of magical time-travelling furniture deciding my fate 125 years before I was born, but here's the thing: the families from which my mother is descended—the Everests and the Lathams on her father's side, and the Modes and the Colletts on her mother's side—came to Canada in the early to mid-1800s. The Everests of England eventually settled in Toronto and established a grocery store (they became city people), while the Lathams of Ireland and the Modes of Scotland established farms elsewhere in Ontario (they became country people). My mother believes the Colletts came from England but knows nothing else about her mother's maternal line.

I was born in Toronto and lived there for my first three years, then spent the next three decades living in large towns and cities like Trenton, Cobourg, Kingston, and Vancouver. No matter where I lived, though, I felt a distinct longing for the country: for a farm, fresh air, fields, and woods. But just as I didn't see the writing on Granny's chest, I didn't pay attention to my (deeply buried) rural roots.

And those roots have a history—and a magic—of their own.

Life is Short: Live in the Country

1

Starry, Starry Night

⸺ ⸱•⸱ ⸺

"You're not in Vancouver anymore," my father kept saying. As if I hadn't noticed cows in the field next to the house, screens on the windows, and tractors loaded with huge bales of hay rumbling through the village—a village which, in May 2002, boasted one business each for money, mail, hardware, gifts, antiques, and pharmaceuticals, plus a couple of restaurants and two gas stations. The entire village offered the same amenities as the six-block radius of my neighbourhood in Vancouver.

When I packed myself and my dog into the car and drove across Canada to my parents' summer house on the east coast, I needed to clear my head, mend my broken heart, and rediscover my dreams. My tongue got tangled up in all the clichés but I quickly discovered the root of my unhappiness: I was not cut out for city living.

At the time, according to the 2001 census, roughly 80 percent of Canadians lived in cities, with almost half of those in the eight largest: Toronto, Montreal, Vancouver, Ottawa-Hull, Calgary, Edmonton, Quebec City, or Winnipeg. When that census was taken, I was living in Canada's third-largest city with almost two million other people.

There are reasons so many seek out large urban centres: cities make you believe in possibilities, in dreams. There are so many choices, from what neighbourhood to live in to where to eat dinner, to what fabulous job you'll land. I liked having Vancouver as my return address; I relished my mother's envy of my proximity to Granville Island Market, my husband biked to work, and we were able to sit on our rooftop deck in mid-January. All our friends had well-paying, interesting jobs, I had an entertaining job as a radio newscaster, and I had wonderful friends.

The longer I lived there, though, the more difficult it became to find breathing space. The expense, the crowds, and the crime wore me down. My husband and I would never be able to afford a house with a backyard, my car was stolen twice, and the stench of urine in the exit stairwell of the movie theatre downtown made me gag. Eventually, not even my wonderful friends could distract me from my growing dislike of city life.

When the marriage that had taken me to BC ended, my exit plan was simple: Pugwash. The first and only place I thought of escaping to was a small fishing village in rural Nova Scotia. I didn't want my own apartment on the other side of Vancouver (I couldn't have afforded it on my radio salary, anyway) and I didn't want to move to Toronto or New York to reinvent myself in a different big city. I wanted to be as far away from crowds, crime, and conspicuous consumption as possible. I wanted space—green space and blue space—as far as my eyes could see.

Others may simply have painted their walls green and blue, bought a ficus tree for their living room, then spent more time hiking in the woods. But there was a siren call for me: a revolving light and foghorn I could not ignore, beaming at me from the opposite coast.

As with all life-changing moves, I went through a period of adjustment: where were the sidewalks? The streetlights? The stores? I wasn't used to walking on the road. I wasn't used to fields separating houses, or driving into the village for every errand. There was no yoga studio, no coffee shop on every corner. Still in big-city mode, every time I parked my car, I'd clamp an anti-theft device called a "club" onto my steering wheel. My father would admonish, "You don't need that: you're not in Vancouver anymore." Eventually, I chucked the club in the trunk. It was still a few months before I stopped locking my car doors altogether (only after I realized I didn't even need a key to the house because nothing was ever locked). It was quite a change from Vancouver, where bicycles and barbecues kept outside had to be padlocked—not because of the *possibility* of their being stolen, but the certainty.

My biggest adjustment from city to country living wasn't the space and the quiet; it was the night. Especially driving at night. I'd been driving since I was sixteen years old, on busy streets with traffic lights and construction, on four- and six-lane highways, in rush hours across the country. But nothing prepared me for how dark the night was the first time I drove down our lane and onto Pugwash Point Road. Once I left the bright yard light behind my headlights cut a path through the murky blackness, but beyond those two thin streams of light, there was nothing. No streetlights, no line on the road…nothing but black. The blazing yard light on each property served as a momentary marker, a brief illumination of a house, until I was plunged back into the blinding darkness.

Yet this very darkness revealed the soul I'd lost in the city. After ten years of city life, of highways, apartment buildings, and office towers, suddenly it was cows, fields, water, and a great big sky that surrounded me.

Green and blue space during the day.

Glittering, black space during the night.

From my rooftop patio in Vancouver, I might be able to see a dozen stars if I cupped my hands around my eyes to block the city lights. Mostly, I looked out over the artificial lights sprawling beneath me instead of above me.

One warm night in July, a few months after I'd arrived at the top of this hill in the middle of a field on a point of land jutting into the Northumberland Strait, I let our two dogs out for their bedtime pee. The yard was dark and quiet. The only sound came from the dogs' paws on the gravel driveway. I still wasn't used to this kind of silence, the kind not filled with sirens and horns, air brakes, delivery trucks dropping their ramps on the asphalt, voices of people walking by on the street.

In June, when the spring peepers were singing their tiny amphibian hearts out, my nine-year-old city dog, Maggie, would not leave the front porch. This dog had faced down nippy terriers at the dog park, manoeuvred with ease through crowded streets and crosswalks, and didn't even jump when a bus squealed and puffed pulling up to a curb. This tough old dog was scared by the symphony of invisible peepers and the dark. For a city dog, the space, silence, and darkness was overwhelming.

Or perhaps Maggie just enjoyed sitting in the dark listening to the silence, breathing in the sheer wonderfulness of being here like I was learning to. I was trying to slow down, open my eyes and ears, and notice long-forgotten details about the world, this place, and myself.

Standing on the back porch while the dogs wandered off into the yard to sniff and squat, I tipped my head back and looked up at the clear night sky.

Stars. Thousands of stars.

The longer I looked, the more I saw, and the more defined the galaxy became. This was the same sky I'd stood under a thousand kilometres ago, but now my only thought was, *This sky makes me believe in infinite possibilities.*

Standing under that sky with a dream in my pocket and an ache in my heart, that thought popped into my head fully formed and clear, without gut-clawing fear, isolation, or self-doubt. Instead, that simple surrender filled me with awe and excitement.

For the past few weeks, I'd been reading a collection of writings by Madeleine L'Engle, a prolific American Christian author. It was divided into short excerpts, and I read one passage each night at bedtime. The reading from the night before was from a book she had written in 1983, when I was thirteen years old and at the height of our best vacations in Pugwash. In that excerpt, I had learned that the word "disaster" is made up of two words: *dis*, meaning separation, and *aster*, meaning star. "So disaster is separation from the stars," L'Engle wrote. "Such separation is disaster indeed. When we are separated from the stars, the sea, each other, we are in danger of being separated from God."

Now, staring up at the night sky, thinking of the origins of the word "disaster," I suddenly realized that the toxicity of a marriage between two incompatible people had permeated my entire life, including my work, my friendships, and my ambitions. When a person is only happy when she is alone, walking her dog on an empty beach at seven o'clock on Saturday morning, her life has become a disaster. There was only one thing to do: go searching for peace in the only place I knew I'd find it. As with any search, you end up discovering things you didn't even know you were looking for. Like stars.

The vast and limitless sky, with so much space about which we know so little, did not make me feel small, insignificant, sad, or lost. It made me feel wide open and connected. It made me believe in myself again, in my dreams and hopes, my future. In infinite possibilities. For someone who, at the age of thirty-two, had left a marriage and a job and moved across the country with no idea of what to do next, that was quite a vast and limitless thought.

In that moment, I felt like I'd left the "dis-aster" of my life behind. That east coast sky revealed no sign of what lay ahead, just the promise that as long as I remembered to look up at the stars, I would always know where I belonged.

2

The Americans Have Arrived

———— ·‥· ————

𝒜 fter all his meticulous research, including an extensive tour around Nova Scotia, former New York resident Ron Maron was not prepared for the wind. "That was the surprise coming up here," he told me while we chatted in the house overlooking Wallace Bay where he now lives with his wife, Mary. "I never registered that when you live on a peninsula out in the ocean, it's going to be windy."

That's what you get when one of the requirements for your retirement home is "on the water" and instead of choosing Florida or the French Riviera, you choose the east coast of Canada. Of all the places in the world to retire, how did a psychotherapist and an elementary school teacher from Buffalo, New York, end up in Wallace? As is often the case, it was personal: Ron's maternal grandfather was born in Toronto but moved to the United States at age seventeen.

"He raised me till I was about ten," Ron said. "He's the one who taught me to love Canada; he took me on fishing trips throughout Ontario. We vacationed at Pigeon Lake, near Peterborough, and took trips along the back roads." He leans back in his kitchen chair as he thinks about his childhood. "Living in Buffalo, so close to the border, I imagine I'd been to Canada well over a hundred times. My grandfather also taught me that there are things about Canadian culture that are better than United States culture," he added. "Like focusing on people rather than defense budgets."

When it came time to retire, Ron and Mary were guided by something a friend had once told Mary: you don't retire *from* something, you retire *to* something.

"We decided we could go wherever we wanted to go and live wherever we wanted to be," Mary said. "We felt a pull to Canada because of Ron's grandfather, so we looked into becoming permanent residents. We didn't want to do seasonal; we really wanted to be in [one] place, to put down roots."

Even though they had owned a cabin in upstate New York, a place surrounded by woods, they were ready for a change—some place surrounded by water. And not just any water, either; Buffalo sat on the shores of Lake Erie, so Mary says they already knew what life was like on a lake.

"We were really looking for something different and to live by the ocean was quite different," she remembered. That meant Ron and Mary had two coastal provinces to choose from: Nova Scotia or British Columbia.

In April 2003, the Marons flew to Nova Scotia and drove their rented car all over the province—including Cape Breton—in one week. The topography and "wonderful" people convinced them they belonged in Nova Scotia. They didn't even visit the west coast; their decision was made.

According to Mary, the defining moment in that vacation came during dinner at a restaurant in Dartmouth. "Ron told our waiter that we were considering moving to Nova Scotia and he asked if we should do that," she said. "She didn't just flippantly come up with something; she really gave it some thought before she answered. She said, 'It's the people.' That was the reason to move to Nova Scotia."

Ron asked that question over and over during the whirlwind vacation and received the same answer every time. The Marons didn't fully understand until they experienced Maritime hospitality first hand.

In the fall of 2004, almost three years after they'd begun the application process to emigrate to Canada, the Marons were accepted as permanent residents. Mary retired from teaching, they sold their house and cabin in Buffalo. They packed up the station wagon with personal belongings and their shih-tzu, Tiffy, and headed north. In January. With no house waiting for them.

"We were ready to have an adventure," Mary laughed as she recalled their big move in early 2005. "Not too many people are looking for houses in January! Wherever we stopped, we met the most wonderful realtors. They weren't just trying to make a sale."

On their first trip to Nova Scotia, Ron and Mary hadn't driven as far as Cumberland County. This time, though, they were coming from Maine and had to drive right through it in order to get to the South Shore.

"I'd seen this house in Wallace on the internet," said Ron, "so we went to see it. It was one of the first houses we saw but we had fifty, sixty more houses we wanted to see."

By March, the couple had decided the South Shore was too crowded and touristy and decided to put in an offer on the first house they'd viewed—a big house on a sprawling, well-maintained lot on Route 6 on the eastern edge of Wallace, Cumberland County.

"We didn't find this house; the house found us," Ron explained. "Mary wanted a nice kitchen. I wanted a small lawn…so Mary got her kitchen," he chuckled, since he has three acres of lawn to mow. Most of all, the house, with its sweeping view of Wallace Bay, fulfills their wish to be on the water.

Although Mary and Ron already felt welcomed by the friendly Maritimers they met, they were shocked by what happened the day they moved in at the end of March.

"Some of our stuff that was in storage arrived in a big moving van—a huge semi. The driver looked at our long driveway and knew he couldn't even make the turn to get into it, and [even] if he did, how would he get back out again?" Mary said. "He had to park on the road. So there was that long driveway and all of our things had to get to the house. Well, we found out right away what nice neighbours we had because right next door—"

"—Remember, we hadn't met any of these people yet," Ron interjected.

"We call them the two Shirleys," Mary explained, referencing one woman who lives next door and one across the road. "They had been talking to each other and were very anxious about what these Americans were doing. Their first thought wasn't, 'What's going on?' but, 'What can we do to help?' So Shirley next door called and asked if we'd like to borrow her pickup truck. The moving guy saw me driving it over and gave a huge sigh of relief," Mary laughed.

Mary doesn't think Maritimers realize just how friendly they are. Yet she and Ron had offered their new neighbours—and the entire hamlet of Wallace—everything Maritimers love: the chance to satisfy their curiosity and the chance to offer the solution to a problem. Information and assistance are the twin support beams of rural Nova Scotia life.

Mary hopped into the pickup truck and from that moment on, the lifelong suburbanite embraced country living. She learned to drive a four-wheeler, took up snowshoeing in the winter, nurtured a beautiful flower garden, and watched the wildlife traipse through her yard. She savoured the space that had tidal water on one side and woods on the other.

Thanks to his Canadian-born grandfather, Ron knew the two rules of getting along in the country: one, never lie; and two, always do what you say you're going to do.

"Those are the country mantras you have to live by," he told Mary.

But Ron and Mary weren't the kind of city people—or the kind of Americans—who needed to repeat a mantra in order to fit in. They easily settled into Wallace because they were the same as their neighbours. In fact, one realtor told Ron if she didn't know he was from Buffalo, she would've sworn he was born and raised a Maritimer.

Which is why the pact the couple had made when they first arrived in Nova Scotia—"If no one likes us, that's okay because we really, really care about each other"—was never tested. Mary says they've never regretted moving to rural Nova Scotia.

Ron admitted he misses some of the food available from Buffalo's vibrant ethnic communities, but "It's all about trade-offs," Mary said. "We miss the ethnic food, but now we have so much [fresh] fish."

Mary's mother died less than six months after the Marons moved to Canada, and Mary went back to Buffalo by herself for the funeral. When she returned to Wallace, she had a profound realization: "I was home now. Already, in five months."

Remember their original desire to put down roots as part of their retirement? Four years after moving to Nova Scotia, Ron and Mary became Canadian citizens.

"We could have remained permanent citizens but for me, it was rounding out the whole thing," Mary explained. "Our citizenship ceremony was at the Maritime Museum [of the Atlantic in Halifax]. Going through that ceremony and looking around at the other people in that room made me realize that these people had come to Canada from all over the world and that everybody had a story to tell. It was a very welcoming feeling that day."

It also made Mary realize how fortunate she and Ron were with their immigration experience; it was one that happened by choice, not forced by circumstances.

"We could go back any time we wanted to our home country but some of those people there with us could never do that," Mary remarked.

Thankfully—and, perhaps, miraculously—the Marons have never wondered about roads not taken, or different coasts not explored.

"We absolutely love it here," Mary said. "We entered into this as something we wanted to do; it was a very conscious decision. It's part of life's adventure for us and it continues to be that way. We never know where it's going to lead but it's been absolutely wonderful so far."

Ron, ever the therapist, provided a ranking of the best life decisions he's ever made, and the move to Wallace was in the top three: "The first best decision I've ever made was to marry Mary," he said. "The second best was to go to college. The third best was to move here."

3

Shit (and the Weather) Happens

⸻ ⋯ ⸻

Don't tell anyone in the Maritimes I said this, but I don't really care about the weather. When I lived in Vancouver, my mother pointed out that I rarely talked about it.

"I think you're the only person in the world who doesn't care about the weather," she observed from her home in southern Ontario.

I hadn't ever given it much thought, but she was right: it never occurred to me to ask how cold it was in Ontario, or tell her it had been raining for three days straight on the west coast. What did it matter? Perhaps my upbringing helped shape my attitude: I didn't grow up on a farm, I wasn't a skier or boater, nor was I involved in any activity affected by precipitation. One can read regardless of the weather.

My only hang-up about the weather is sunshine: I can't work inside on nice days. When we were kids spending our summers on Rice Lake north of Cobourg, Ontario, my mother would tell my sister and me, "You shouldn't be inside on such a nice day—go do something outside." This may explain why I write best on rainy and snowy days.

I'll tell you one thing: not talking about the weather makes me a terrible conversationalist. When you think about it, weather is our small talk, which makes sense because there is always something to talk about, but people in the Maritimes take it to a whole new level. By people, I mean my husband. Right after he says hello, whether he's called or answered the phone, he makes a comment about the weather.

"Coming in cold, Dad."

"Nice day out, Dave."

"It put down a lot of rain last night."

In fact, he even gets twitchy when denied the opportunity to talk about weather. I once heard him mention how hot it was right at the end of a phone conversation, as if to get it in before the call ended. What I love most about this obsession is how it states the obvious. My husband will stand at the sliding glass doors overlooking the front deck and yard, staring through a sheet of rain, and say into the phone, "Really coming down," as if the person on the other end—likely his father or neighbour—isn't looking at the exact same scene.

"I wouldn't doubt it's put down four inches of rain already," he'll say.

His father, who lives less than a kilometre away, will argue: "No, it's rained six inches already, Dwayne."

As if that wasn't amusing enough, my husband *does* have some delightful weather adages I've learned to trust. In any season when he announces, "There's a sun dog to the left [or right] of the sun," that yellow spot means I can count on a big storm within three days. "When the new moon goes down south of west, we're going to have warmer-than-normal weather for two weeks," he will tell me. On a wet morning, he might look out the window and say, "If the drops are hanging off the tree branches, it means the rain isn't over yet."

My favourite is the circle around the moon. The first time Dwayne pointed this out was a clear, moonlit night a month before our wedding.

"There's going to be a lot of rain in three days," he told me when he came inside after smoking his last cigarette of the day.

"How on earth do you know that?" I scoffed. "Did an owl tell you?"

"There is a circle around the moon with three stars inside it. The number of stars inside the circle is the number of days before we get a big storm."

I soon learned his old-world predictions are nothing to be mocked because they're accurate; apparently, his circle around the moon predicted White Juan in February 2004, much to the astonishment of his co-workers. The aphorisms are just like weather: created by nature, uncontrolled by humans. In a world where locations, likes and preferences, meals, and workouts are recorded—and where storms are tracked weeks in advance—to have the natural world operating above and beyond our control is exactly what we need. In our universe, weather remains supreme ruler no matter how many attempts we make to overthrow its regime.

I may not use weather as small talk or care how I could be impacted (unless it knocks out the power) but it doesn't mean I'm not interested in weather in general. There is one thing about weather that excites me: microclimates. I first heard the term used by my friend, Kim, when we worked together at a radio station in Vancouver. She would leave her home in North Vancouver in a snowstorm, drive through rain in Vancouver, and arrive to dry roads and the sun coming up over the station in Richmond, just thirty kilometres south.

Sound familiar, Maritimers? Rain in Halifax, blizzard on the Cobequid Pass. Fifteen degrees in Yarmouth, minus two in Amherst. How many microclimates exist within Cape Breton alone?

For someone who doesn't talk about the weather, I've managed to write quite a bit about it. It's an unpopular sentiment but I think I can admit the truth: I love weather. I love snowstorms and thunderstorms. I love wind (although not at night) and hot, sunny days, and rainbows. I love seeing the spill of clouds across the shore that says rain is coming quickly. I don't even mind the "red bar of doom" that appears on the Environment Canada website before a big storm. Weather is *exciting*. It might not be that I love weather so much as I love variety—waking up each day not knowing what beautiful meteorological event is going to occur.

I love weather; I just don't like talking about it. And I really don't like the way everyone else talks about it. Perhaps the tiny slice of my genetic pie that has "farming" in it means I look to the sky and accept whatever precipitation is (or isn't) coming my way.

It makes me wonder if the migration to cities left rural stoicism behind. Weather used to be whatever you saw out the window or windshield, and you dealt with it as you went along. It was no big deal because there was nothing you could do to change it. Now, twenty-four-hour weather networks and around-the-clock newscasts mean weather gets overhyped and overexposed, so we overreact. When we start panicking about a run-of-the-mill, fifteen-centimetre snowstorm a week before it arrives, we've lost perspective. In Canada, we should expect snow during winter. Heck, in the Maritimes, we should expect snow in May!

We do the same with rain. One day of rain and people start commenting, "Good weather if you're a duck." To be fair, six straight days of rain—or the winter of 2015—are clear and accepted grounds for whining about all the precipitation. But there are people who are seriously put out by the weather: people who seem to take it very personally when it rains on a Tuesday in June—or November—and snows on Christmas Day—or in March.

Some weather lovers, however, are pushing back. There is such a thing as the Cloud Appreciation Society in the UK, and its manifesto opens: "We believe clouds are unjustly maligned and life would be immeasurably poorer without them." The society has a website and Facebook page, and nearly forty thousand members. Clearly, a specific society for the appreciation of clouds resonates with a lot of people.

"People think of clouds as things that get in the way," explained society founder Gavin Pretor-Pinney in a 2013 TED (Technology, Entertainment, and Design) Talk called *Cloudy with the Chance of Joy*. "They think of clouds as annoying, frustrating obstructions."

I find this incredibly odd since clouds are in the sky. How can they be in our way? But then I remember: they are responsible for rain and snow. Particularly snow. Which is, if you listen to the radio, watch television, or follow social media, *the end of civilization as we know it.*

There is so much beauty and variety in our weather, we should celebrate it, not abhor it. Even the winter of 2015 was exciting and interesting. What is the point of complaining about the onslaught of snow, how slowly it's cleared away, or how long it lasts? We've grown used to the instant gratification of computers and technology and begun to think people and their plows are capable of the same instantaneous action. We've lost perspective on how long it takes to physically clear a metre of snow, and have created unrealistic expectations about how well a small machine can scrape away layers of ice. How soon until we expect snow to be cleared before it even reaches the ground?

One Saturday morning a couple of winters ago, as I waited in my car outside the pharmacy in Oxford, an older woman with a rollator (a four-wheeled walker) manoeuvred along the snow-covered sidewalk. Two centimetres of snow had fallen the night before and she was pushing hard to keep her wheels moving. I didn't think how outrageous it was that the sidewalks weren't perfectly bare; rather, I thought, *rollators should come with snow tires.*

Driving uptown, I spotted another woman with a rollator tromping to Tim Hortons. I admired both women for their old-school determination; they were not letting a bit of snow get in the way of their errands. They were too busy power-rolling to shake their fists at the clouds and shout, "Curse you, annoying obstructions! How dare you?"

What's the point? We all know shit happens. So, too, does weather. Every minute of every day.

Despite the variety of weather, it doesn't really change. We are the ones who have changed. We have gone from calm—or resigned—acceptance of six straight days of crop-ruining rain or back-to-back blizzards to freaking out five days ahead of a forecasted snowfall. We use fancy meteorological terms like "polar vortex" to describe an average -25 degree day in mid-January.

Let's try to be more like those two women on that snowy Saturday morning, full of determination and spirit and muscle power. They didn't care about the weather, and they certainly weren't taking it personally. When those two women reached their destinations, they could feel proud of themselves for creating a new winter sport: free-style rollator cross.

Let's be more like Halifax radio-host-turned-author Stephanie Domet, who was still hosting CBC Radio One's *Mainstreet* when she created the idea of "storm chips": a stockpile of potato chips for hunkering down and making it through a blizzard. That's the attitude we need when it comes to the weather: common sense in the face of insurmountable snowdrifts.

4

Give Us This Day Our Daily Egg

An hour ago, my husband told me he was going to check on the chickens and rabbits. He hasn't come back inside yet. I can see our yellow coop from the kitchen window and I don't see him lying in a snowdrift so I pull on my winter coat, hat, and red Bog boots, and head outside.

Pushing open the door of the chicken coop, I am greeted by the humid aroma of fur, feathers, straw, and poop. My husband is sitting on a bale of straw.

"Here you are," I say, sitting down beside him.

We sit side by side without speaking, and inhale the warm, slightly pungent air. Our three rabbits rustle in the straw around the hollowed-out log they use as a burrow, and the *berk-berk-berk* of twenty hens floats over to us from the other side of the partition. Occasionally, our rooster hollers.

"Hey, Brewster," I call back.

We sit there for a long time. It's so warm and peaceful we don't want to leave. There is something very soothing about the clucking sound from a flock of contented hens. If any of my Ontario friends could see me now, they would laugh. They would laugh because they are happy for me; they don't get this whole Nova Scotia country thing, but secretly I think they want to. They aren't the only ones surprised to find me sitting in a chicken coop.

The origins of this moment are found in a list.

It was the summer of 2006, and I was on a month-long vacation at my family's summer house in Pugwash. It was the first summer since my father's Alzheimer's diagnosis we hadn't come down in May, but with Dad living in a nursing home and Mum recovering from cancer surgery, we had postponed the annual tradition.

But my parents' dog, Lisa, had also been recently diagnosed with cancer, and Mum thought the dog should have one last walk on the red sand. She packed me and the two dogs—thirteen-year-old Lisa and three-year-old Stella—off to Pugwash for a break before her chemotherapy and radiation treatments began.

I arrived in mid-July and it was strange to find the old, renovated farmhouse already warm inside, instead of the dry cold of early May. As soon as I set foot in that house, peace enveloped me. After months of the shallow breathing of worry, I began to breathe deeply. When I woke in the morning, I didn't feel anxious or fearful. I walked the dogs on the beach, had breakfast, drank coffee, and gazed at the green fields and turquoise water. All the tension and worry associated with life back home in Ontario evaporated like dew in the summer sunshine.

I unpacked the bag full of my most important supplies. This respite was a time to catch up on reading, do some painting, writing, and all those creative pursuits that take a back seat when you are a caregiver. I opened a book of writing exercises by Julia Cameron, and sat at the dining room table cutting words and images out of magazines and pasting them on poster board to create a collage of my "consciousness at this time." While this might seem a potentially distressing endeavour for someone taking care of two parents with life-threatening illnesses, I completed it while looking over fields of wildflowers to a sparkling harbour, and somehow my poster ended up brimming with hope, happiness, cookies, and cows.

The second exercise, however, was different.

Cameron, who had been living in New York City when she penned this book, wrote, "Each of us has a different idea of sophistication. Each of us has certain items that speak to us as tokens of success…List 25 things that represent to you sophistication and success." By the time I reached twelve, I was stuck. By this time, I was curled up in a chair in the living room, gazing out the sliding doors to our backyard. I soon realized what it was about the list that put me off.

I drew a heavy line through a tuxedo, a glass of champagne, and a trip to Italy and wrote "A chicken coop in the backyard." From some deep, unknown place inside me, a place only this house on Pugwash Point could reach, my inner, long-suppressed country girl asserted herself.

A week later, an equally amazing and unexpected thing happened: I went on a blind date. For this country girl wannabe and a Nova Scotia country boy, it was love at first sight (or rather, bite, since I knew halfway through supper). A few weeks later, just before I was due to return to Ontario, I said to this man who happened to live on seventy-two acres, "You have lots of room here for chickens."

"I would love to have chickens," he replied.

Actually, *that* could be the moment I truly fell in love with him. You see? Birds of a feather want to have eggs together. I was destined to marry the man who could make my dream of a chicken coop in the backyard a reality.

As our first wedding anniversary approached, we built a coop as pretty as a small cottage. We placed chairs next to the outdoor pen and watched the hens as they puttered around, and gathered eggs for friends eager to pay $2.50 per dozen. "Why chickens?" everyone seemed to ask. There's only this answer: chickens are fascinating! Some scientists believe domestic chickens date back ten thousand years. There are nineteen billion domestic chickens worldwide.

The expression "raising your hackles" refers to the hackle feathers on the back of a rooster's neck, which he raises to make himself look bigger. The fear of chickens is called alektoraphobia.

∽⌒∾ ⊃•⊂ ⌒∾

It was my fear of big feet and swishing tails that made me decide seven-pound chickens were the perfect introduction to animal husbandry. Surely I could handle something small and light and feathery.

One afternoon, my husband, whose boyhood chores included tending 150 hens, said, "I've never watched a hen give itself a sand bath before." He then proceeded to demonstrate exactly how she twists and dips one shoulder, then the next. I stood watching in amazement. When the chickens had first arrived, Dwayne told me the only things they do are "shit and lay eggs." Suddenly, he was as enamoured with the chickens as his city-raised wife who'd always longed for livestock.

During a conversation with a woman who had just moved to our area from Halifax, I mentioned I had chickens and she exclaimed, "You have chickens?!" in the same way I would say, "You won a million dollars?!" I appreciated her enthusiasm because I feel the same way.

But not everyone sees the sophistication in my red Bog boots and wire egg basket. "You're a loon," my friend Jennifer tells me. We're on the phone, me in my cozy wood-heated house surrounded by fields, she in her lovely home in the Bloor West Village of Toronto where the houses are built very close to each other. She talks about her two young children while I talk about my twenty chickens; neither of us fully understands what the other is experiencing. She's breastfeeding her six-month-old son while I rave about the delight of reaching under the feathery skirt of a hen for a warm egg.

So these chickens are a symbol. They are proof I have succeeded—finally—in love and in life. Wearing barn boots and pitching poopy straw into a garbage can, pouring feed into a bucket, and lugging water from the outside tap, I am as sophisticated as Jennifer walking along Bloor Street pushing her son in a stroller and buying eggs from the grocery store.

When I still lived in Ontario, I enjoyed many visits with Jennifer. I loved riding the subway to the stop nearest her home then walking past all the little stores on Bloor Street selling everything from fruits and vegetables to lingerie and socks. One afternoon, I glanced in the window of a shoe store and saw the most fabulous pair of red leather boots. They were sexy yet comfortable and surprisingly affordable. They went with everything. When I wore them, I felt confident and cosmopolitan.

Right now, those fabulous red boots are shoved in the back of my closet because they're no good to me now; they definitely weren't meant for tromping across the yard to a little yellow chicken coop. No matter how our lives have diverged in the twenty years since we met at university, Jennifer and I are still the same shoe size. I think I'll mail those boots back to where they belong.

5

A Country Woman
Carries On

ꝰ———···———ꝰ

*J*ane Purdy takes a white bowl covered in plastic wrap out of the fridge and brings it to her kitchen table. She hands me a spoon. I dip it into the thick golden jelly and taste it.

"That's so good," I tell her, pleasantly surprised since I didn't know what to expect. "It tastes like honey."

This is Jane's dandelion jelly, made from the flowers growing in the front yard of the Williamsdale home she's lived in since 1985. Jane, who I know through church, is the epitome of a country woman: she grows a large garden, preserves most of it, and works in the blueberry fields around her home. She is strong, capable, and courageous in the face of tragedy and challenge. But as I'm sitting at her kitchen table, I don't yet know those facets of her life; I'm here because she once mentioned she bottles tomatoes and I want to learn how to do it.

"I picked up a *Country Woman* magazine one day and it had recipes with dandelions," Jane explains. "There was a salad using dandelion greens and this dandelion jelly. It didn't look hard so I thought, 'There's all kinds of dandelions this year, I'm going to try this.'"

It was perhaps the easiest harvest she'd ever made. She picked enough dandelion flowers from her front lawn to make a batch, which she says turned out pretty well. She made a second batch to offer as a novelty item at the United Church Women (UCW) sale at the Collingwood fire hall, where she sold a few bottles because people were curious.

"It was just an experiment," admits Jane. "I have a fascination with recipes and I've always collected them. I'm the worst one, when it comes time for a sale, for trying something new. I know I'm not the only one but I'll try something new, see how it turns out. That was one aspect of this, that it was a new recipe and I was curious to see what a jelly made with dandelion flowers would be like."

This curiosity and fearlessness led her to search out a recipe for a wine jelly with garlic and rosemary that she used to buy at a farmers' market but couldn't get anymore. She was confident enough in her ability—after all, she'd just whipped up two successful batches of dandelion jelly—to assume she could do it.

"It worked out fine," she smiles.

Jane wasn't born and raised in the rural community where she's lived for over thirty years; she married into Williamsdale and the long-established Purdy family. Jane's father was in the military and she was born in Halifax while he was stationed there. By the time she was a teenager, she'd lived in Ontario, France, and Germany, returning to Nova Scotia for her father's final posting before he retired. That's when the family moved to Collingwood where his parents lived.

Although Jane knew Gordon Purdy through school, it wasn't until they had graduated from high school and Jane was living and working in Amherst that Gordon asked her out; a year later they married and eventually had a daughter, Tiffany.

Like so many country women, Jane learned the art of preserving from her mother, Audrey Nix, who lives next door.

"After I was married, I guess it felt like country life to do preserves. We always had a garden; it was up behind my mother-in-law's place. Muriel would buy the seed and we would plant the garden. We grew enough to feed the three of us. She didn't use a lot of the fresh vegetables like beans and beets and peas but I would freeze them to use through the winter."

Although preserving wasn't part of my upbringing, my mother did teach me to make strawberry jam so I understand completely when Jane talks about the sweetest sound to a canner's ears: "That snap when the jar is sealing is so satisfying. I think it brings joy to know you're going to have something that tastes so much nicer in the winter than stuff you buy in the store."

There are those who complain that homemade preserves are too expensive when compared to grocery store prices…but of course they are! Anyone who makes jams, jellies, pickles, or salsa is doing 100 percent the work; the price includes Jane on her hands and knees in the yard collecting dandelion flowers and bent over in the garden individually picking tomatoes and cucumbers. Let's be honest: the true argument against home preserving is the time and effort. With satisfaction as the payoff, it's worth spending a couple of evenings washing, sterilizing, and bottling to enjoy the taste of "fresh" produce all winter.

Jane believes the art of home preserves is making a comeback. "I think more people are getting into it. With the price of groceries and products, I think more people are doing it again."

Despite the resurgence in rural ways of life, it's not reflected in the community. Jane says the (very rural) area she's lived in since she was thirteen years old has changed. "There was so much industry, so many families who ran businesses here back then," she recalls. "People started moving into town or they moved away to get work. Now most of the recreation activities are gone from our community. People have to go to Oxford or Amherst for those activities. They live here but they aren't part of the community because they travel so much. There's nothing to draw people together."

The local church congregation tried, Jane says, by hosting card and game nights but people just weren't interested. Like canning and preserving, gathering as a community to play games, share potluck, or go to church is no longer the expected way of life.

"You can only do so much until you feel like you're beating your head against the wall. I think the internet and television has taken over so much, people don't talk to each other anymore. And there aren't a lot of small children in our community anymore," Jane adds. "We exist here; we don't mingle like we used to."

In 2014, the small congregation attending Millvale United Church just down the road from Jane's home made the difficult decision to close and sell the building.

"For the older generation who had gone to that church when they were small, it was difficult for them because that was a way of life for them. Every Sunday, they attended church and supported that church through fundraisers or UCW group. It was hard to see the church deteriorating, but we knew even if we fixed it up there was no way we'd be able to continue because there was no generation coming up behind us to look after it."

At least the church was sold to a young man who grew up in the area and attended Sunday school there. He renovated the old church for his personal use as a cabin (commonly referred to in rural Nova Scotia as a "camp").

"I'm happy to see the church being used as opposed to tearing it down or seeing it sitting there rotting," Jane says.

A large grey tabby wanders into the kitchen. "That's Blueberry," Jane laughs. "He came from next door."

Next door is the Purdy Resources blueberry operation, one of Cumberland County's most successful family-owned businesses.

"The boys were feeding him in the shed through blueberry season so they called him Shed," Jane tells me as I pat the friendly tabby. "They asked Muriel, my mother-in-law, if she wanted the cat in the house but she didn't think so until she heard that one of the boys was going to take him home. She ended up giving him to my daughter." Tiffany gave him the appropriate—and much cuter—name Blueberry.

Jane was married to Muriel's son, Gordon, who passed away in 2008. Although he was undergoing treatment for cancer, Gordon's death was unexpected and traumatic. Their daughter was in her first year at agriculture college and both women struggled to cope, but they got through it together. There was a time for mourning and then there was a time for continuing the work Gordon enjoyed. Following the example of her mother-in-law (who was widowed in the 1980s but kept the family business going), Jane took over her husband's responsibilities when she inherited his land. She'd worked alongside him since their daughter was born but with his death, she became the farmer. Tiffany followed her mother's lead.

"She would come home in July and she'd take the harvester and tear it all apart and put the parts in it," Jane says, "then we put the machine back together. She'd work on the back for a couple of years then there was one year I couldn't get a driver so I looked at her and said she would run the harvester that year. Gordon's brother, who lives on the other side of my mother, has a machine so we pick together. I have six fields to pick and he has one, so he picks with me and I pick with him."

This is what I admire about Jane, her mother, her mother-in-law, and any woman who is faced with a major life change: they trust implicitly, maybe at times even desperately, in the knowledge they have gained from life experience, from listening and observing.

Naturally, Jane, who turned fifty-five in 2016, wasn't sure she could handle it. "I just go year to year," she says.

Jane had to give up the vegetable garden after Gordon died because it always came on right at blueberry time. Once she took over the business she was too busy to pick vegetables. "We start picking blueberries [on] the seventh or eighth of August. I leave the house at six-thirty in the morning and I don't return home until eight o'clock at night. We have our breaks and some downtime but that's farming: you've got a certain window to pick those berries so they are the best quality. Some year I might sell the tractor and let others do the picking but that won't happen for a while."

Jane didn't give up doing preserves, however, even though she now buys the ingredients. "I still do pickles and beets and relishes," she says. "And I can fifty pounds of tomatoes for casseroles and soups."

That's what I originally came to talk to Jane about, canning tomatoes, but she's amazed me and inspired me far beyond that.

"I guess I have surprised myself that I've continued to carry on with this," she tells me. "But I didn't have any brothers or sons so I'm used to getting my hands dirty."

Jane Purdy's recipe for dandelion jelly came from an American magazine so let's go with a Canadian version. Here is the recipe Jen Wilson of Dakeyne Farm in the Annapolis Valley posted on her personal blog (dakeynefarm.com) and gave me permission to share:

Ingredients and Supplies

> 2 cups fresh dandelion petals
> 2 cups boiling water
> ¼ cup fresh lemon juice
> 4 cups sugar
> 1 package liquid pectin
> 8 (125 ml) jars and lids
> 1 large stainless steel pot
> Cheesecloth or fine sieve

Method

> Snip tops off dandelions, removing as much green as possible (any green will make the jelly bitter).
> Transfer boiled water to large bowl. Place petals in the water and cover. Allow to infuse for 2 hours.
> Wash and sterilize jars and lids. Set aside.
> Strain infusion through a cheesecloth or fine sieve. Be sure not to squeeze the petals (this will make the jelly cloudy).
> Pour strained liquid in a large stainless steel pot. Discard petals.
> Add sugar and lemon juice. Stir.

> Bring liquid to a rolling boil. Add liquid pectin.
> Boil hard for 1 minute, stirring frequently.
> Remove from heat and skim foam off top.
> Pour liquid into 8 sterilized, 125-ml jars; fill to an eighth of an inch from the top. Wipe rims and screw on lids (finger tight). To seal jars, place in a hot-water bath for 10 minutes.
> Sealed jars will last up to one year in a cool place. Unsealed jars will last up to 3 weeks in the refrigerator. Makes 8 small jars.
> Serve on cream crackers or toast.

6

Faith in the Community

It's amazing how the presence of children in a rural church changes the normally tranquil air inside the sanctuary.

One sunny Sunday morning, there was a double baptism at a local country church I attend periodically: a baby and a toddler from one family, accompanied by their two older sisters. Those four children, with their noise and smiles, transformed the energy of both the sanctuary and regular churchgoers. We sang with more enthusiasm, greeted each other with wider smiles, and chatted a little longer after the service. In fact, everyone seemed almost giddy.

Children at a rural church make a notable difference because they are such a rarity. Against our good sense, against the reality of all other Sundays, they make us feel hopeful. Like they might come back, like things are about to change for the better. Many rural congregations now suffer from low attendance, and it affects the choir loft and the nursery. The older generation is hanging on, but there are no younger members sharing the work. Ministers are performing more funerals than baptisms. The reasons are myriad and each of us has our reasons for not going, but it is a vicious cycle of loss for rural communities.

When I moved to Nova Scotia, I didn't bother seeking out a church to attend. Six years later, though, I ended up providing worship services as a lay leader. At the time, I was working at the local community newspaper and one of my duties was updating the weekly church notices. When I found out one of the United Church pastoral charges (made up of three churches) did not have a regular minister, I offered to help.

I have no formal training or degree, but I was raised in the United Church and am familiar with its doctrine, ethos, and hymn book; I can write, speak, and plan services. And so, with equal amounts anxiety and anticipation, I embarked on what has become the unexpectedly satisfying journey of serving several churches in my area.

It so happens my very first day was Epiphany Sunday. While it is a Christian holy day marking the arrival of the Magi (the wise men) to meet the infant Jesus, generally the word "epiphany" means "a sudden and important manifestation or realization." It's often used to describe scientific breakthroughs and spiritual discoveries, though an epiphany is not so much "eureka!" as a quieter revelation, like a light bulb flickering on. An epiphany comes from suddenly understanding a situation or person from a new perspective.

My church-related epiphany was this: here was a way for me to help rural communities stave off one aspect of their decline a little longer. By working as a lay worship leader and providing a service every Sunday, I am *in service* to these churches and the two-dozen faithful who insist on showing up every Sunday; those churchgoers who persist, who won't give up, and who cling to ways of the past.

These are the very qualities that keep so much of rural Nova Scotia chugging along. But what we value, what we grasp so tightly, can also hold us back. Often, it's resistance to change that keeps young people from sticking around and drives people away from church and rural areas in the first place.

Every so often someone asks me, "Are you thinking of going into the ministry?" I smile and answer, "No, I'm happy with everything I'm doing right now." And I am perfectly happy to provide the occasional worship service that gives dedicated members their day in church. It allows their congregation to survive, even if it's not thriving.

The truth is I see no point in pursuing a degree that will lead to ordination because I don't see there being any full-time church jobs in my area and I refuse to leave in order to find work as hundreds of others have done. One of the three churches in the pastoral charge where I started has already closed, been de-sanctified, and sold. Another pastoral charge may close two of its three churches, essentially orphaning its third vibrant, active congregation. When its vibrant, active members begin to fade, so too will the financial support and that church's role in its seaside community.

There are good reasons people choose not to attend church; I used many of them for six years. On one hand, the failure of churches to adapt, the insistence on clinging to familiar ways, and allowing emotional arguments ("my grandparents were married in this church so nothing should ever change") to inform decisions has hurt attendance. When does sincere dedication become blind stubbornness?

On the other hand, churches can provide so much more to a community than hymns and prayers and sermons on Sunday morning. Members of the churches I attend support the local food bank by donating items each week and filling boxes at Christmastime. They knit prayer shawls for those who are ill, and hats and mittens for the Brunswick Street Mission in Halifax. Women's groups provide lunches for funeral receptions. How many people would remember to collect items for the food bank if they weren't going to church? Who will donate mittens and hats to the homeless if these churches close? Who will provide tea, coffee, sandwiches, and sweets to mourners? The loss of those congregations will have a ripple effect far beyond church doors and county lines.

My work as a lay worship leader has opened my eyes to what "those old and out-of-touch people at church" accomplish year after year. A dozen people, by sheer force of will and faith, are keeping their churches open while doing the work of two dozen. It's not unusual for the same people to remain on the same committee for decades, as no one else is willing—or available—to take their positions.

This pattern is reflected in the surrounding community as well. The commitment of small congregations to their church is the kind of investment every rural area needs from all its residents, not just the same few.

Our rural communities are no longer filled with people in their thirties and forties who are starting families and putting down roots. While that is reflected most obviously in church pews, it's also apparent in the readership of local newspapers, and attendance at local events like pancake suppers, craft shows, and concerts. Whether we're talking about a church or a community, every death is another step closer to emptiness. Everyone under the age of fifty who says, "I've lived here all my life, I wouldn't want to live anywhere else," needs to offer more than lip service to that insistence on staying put. Without involvement and support in stores, on newsstands, in pews, and at service clubs and other volunteer organizations, as well as at festivals and concerts, a community crumbles.

It's fair to ask why we want to maintain large, frequently inaccessible, draughty churches if membership is declining, yet one particular example proved—to me—the necessity of a spiritual gathering place. We instinctively gravitate to places like this when something horrific happens, whether it's a sudden, tragic car accident or the shooting of twenty first-graders at an elementary school.

That shooting in Newtown, Connecticut, on Friday, December 14, 2012, happened the morning of the Pugwash Christmas concert. The concert went ahead as planned—not despite the tragedy, but because of it. The concert is traditionally held at the United Church— the largest—but on that cold December evening, it didn't matter what church you regularly attended. It didn't matter if you didn't go at all, were deeply religious, or only casually spiritual; we gathered as a community of humans with hurting hearts. We arrived quietly, stunned and reeling, and sank onto the quickly filling pews. The enormous Christmas tree, twinkling with lights and ornaments, promised us peace, hope, and joy. The choir looked elegant in white and black, and the costumed children were quietly restless. We needed the sanctuary and familiar comfort provided by that concert in that beautiful, sacred space.

The keyboardist was an elementary school vice-principal and the mother of a grade two student. Already running on the hyper-exhaustion that comes with putting on a community Christmas concert, I'm sure she had not yet processed what happened.

At the end of the concert, the church's minister, Meggin King, spoke the necessary words of comfort and peace—not because we had come seeking answers from God, but because this was the place to be with friends and family for the annual concert. It just happened to be the right place and time. Afterwards, we gathered downstairs for tea, coffee, sandwiches, and sweets. We greeted each other, chatted about Christmas plans, hugged a little tighter, and sat together a little longer.

The concert on December 14, 2012 wasn't a large one in the city where attendees were surrounded by strangers, arriving and leaving without exchanging more than small talk with others; in that rural church basement, we milled around with friends and family. We weren't pretending the shootings in Newtown hadn't happened; we were counting our blessings and trying to find support, encouragement, hope, and joy in the midst of the unbelievable sadness. When churches cease to exist, how will people deal with their worries and grief? Where will they gather to support each other as a community? No matter how many people click "like" on a person's "prayer to heaven" Facebook post, social media can't provide the face-to-face contact of conversation and the heart-to-heart connection of hugs.

This is the heart and soul of a rural community: not the church itself but the spirit of hope and devotion that fills those who enter, whether it's a Sunday service or a Wednesday evening ham supper. This is the heart and soul of a rural community: not the town or village but the spirit of optimism and persistence in the face of apparently insurmountable odds for long-term viability.

The sad truth is, love them or resist them, churches, like the rural communities surrounding them, are no longer the backbone of society. As we lose these spaces, we lose the unique way rural folk exhibit the values of loyalty to their area and neighbours, as well as their single-minded commitment to work together and provide support—whether it's emotional, financial, or spiritual—in times of trouble or celebration.

When my friend Sharon turned sixty, she decided it was time to be baptized at the church in Collingwood where she'd grown up. Invited to take part in the laying on of hands during her baptism, I stood at the front of the church and placed my palm on her head. Betty, in her eighties, an avid quilter and the church's long-time clerk of session, lay her hand on top of mine. As the retired ordained minister (hired specially to perform this sacrament) spoke the formal words of baptism, I felt the energy flowing between the four of us, pulsing with the hope and joy and love that comes with being part of a dedicated, if dwindling, rural church family.

7

By Any Other Name

June Thurber has her paint, brushes, and canvas spread around her when I arrive. She's a member of Mixed Palette—an art group that meets every Thursday morning at the village hall in Pugwash. Despite selling many of her paintings, you won't discover any original Thurbers in local homes; June paints under an alias.

"I use my maiden name, Frauzel," she tells me. "I told my husband at the time that I could have three or four more husbands before I stopped painting. It was only a joke."

Yet she was joking with her second husband.

Now eighty-six with a pacemaker to give her a new lease on life, she's content sharing a two-bedroom apartment with one of her sisters in a small retirement complex. She can paint in front of the south-facing window in the kitchen.

June Thurber is the retired teacher, whose husband, Byard, died twelve years ago.

June Frauzel is the lifelong artist who didn't have time to paint until she retired. In between, there was June Turner, the divorced mother of ten who taught high school English in Pugwash, Nova Scotia.

"Now wipe that look off your face," June commands, ever the stern schoolteacher.

My mouth didn't form an "O" of shock but rather one of awe: June raised ten children on her own while teaching full-time.

"I haven't seen that face in awhile," she adds. "People would ask,"—here she minces her voice—"'And how many children to you have, Mrs. Turner?' and I'd say, 'Ten,' and they'd say 'Oh, isn't that lovely?' but there would be a look of horror in between," she laughs.

"It's not horror, it's amazement," I insist.

"Well, we'll put it down as that."

She began teaching before she got married at age eighteen— "They were desperate for teachers," June says—but the implication seems to be she didn't have much choice about the nuptials, as her first child was born "uncomfortably soon" after the wedding.

Ten births later, older, wiser, and perhaps less afraid of shame as she once was, June decided to leave her husband and take the children. This meant she had to find work to support them all, so she upgraded her teaching credentials by attending teachers' college in Truro. She somehow went to school and raised ten children at the same time. "I was a regular Tillie the Toiler," she remembers.

When it came time to find a job, she applied for elementary, junior, and senior positions. "I even considered going to Labrador so I could pay off my debts. I had a back-breaking load of student loans so I'd threaten the boys: 'Maybe we'll go up north,' I'd say."

I noticed a slight twang when she pronounced "north"; it sounded like "noth."

June knew for sure she wasn't going to Halifax. Even if there were more jobs there, she didn't want her older kids roaming the city streets. She eventually accepted a job in Pugwash teaching high school English, but by the time she and her family had moved to the small fishing village, only six of June's ten children were living at home (the oldest three were on their own and one son living in Vancouver sadly passed away a month after his family arrived in Pugwash). Her still-at-home children ranged in age from six to sixteen.

"It's been a lovely place to live, it really has," June says of Pugwash. "It was like being part of another family here. When we moved there, I bought a mobile home and moved in with the six kids. Someone came over and said, 'You don't know me but I'd like to help. I can babysit for you.' I don't know who it was, and I didn't take her up on her offer. I didn't do any socializing at that time of my life. But I never forgot that. It was more than you'd expect."

Knowing she's not originally from Pugwash and hearing a New England accent every time June says "arm" or "harbour"—and considering June lives in a village on the Northumberland Strait and paints seascapes in her spare time, she says "hah-bah" quite a bit—I ask June where she was born. She chuckles and tells me she grew up on a small farm near Bridgewater. June says the farm was small enough that her father worked other jobs. "It was a good upbringing, a typical farm upbringing with churchgoing parents," she says. "I learned how to milk a cow but I also learned how to avoid it."

She was raised with four brothers and three sisters. "I'm in the middle," she says. "That's the reason I am the way I am."

I've already deduced June is a tough, no-nonsense, practical, plain-speaking woman—a mother and a teacher—but there's nothing mean about her bluntness; she's rather good-natured. It's clear, however, that being tough was necessary for her to succeed. "I never got to be a mother," June says. "My kids were [essentially] raised by Attila the Hun. Now, I have nine best friends but I don't know how because I wasn't a sweet little mother, I can tell you that. They were good years but they were busy."

On one wall of the mobile home hung what she calls a prison worksheet. "With the kids, this one had to do this, this one had to do that, and another one would check it off when it was done. Worked like a dream with Attila the Hun as backup. You couldn't be the soft little mother."

Like any single mother, June had to make it work because she and her kids had to survive. "I can remember when I was home sick one day; I was never sick but I took a couple of sick days a year when I got behind in my corrections. My youngest son, Bill, had come home and I'd made supper. He said, 'Mom, I wish you were home all the time.' We weren't a very demonstrative family," June adds, "but that said a lot."

One of the reasons June retired from teaching in the mid-eighties was the attitudes of her students. "I liked teaching for a long, long while," she says. "It's a hard job if you're doing your job. But kids' attitudes changed. I think mostly when mothers ended up going to work. Kids didn't have a mother at home."

The irony of that statement isn't lost on June. She admits that both she and her children made sacrifices and there wasn't a whole lot of fun.

Her other reason was Byard Thurber. She'd met him through a friend, married him after all her children were out of the house, and wanted to travel with him. They'd been married for twenty-five years when he passed away in 2004.

It's clear Mrs. Turner (a.k.a. June Frauzel, a.k.a. June Thurber) made an impression on the students at Pugwash District High School. She considers it "a wonderful compliment" when grown-up, long-graduated students tell her she wasn't boring. After so many years in Pugwash, where more people know Mrs. Turner than June likely realizes, she remains a legend.

"When my grandkids visit, they can't believe this: I don't carry a parcel out from the post office. If I arrive and say I have a parcel in the car, they go out and get it for me. I've gone into the hospital and before I had the cast on my leg, there were flowers there."

June says she's had offers from people who say, "You've done so much for me, I want to help," and June doesn't have a clue who they are.

"I say I'm going to wear a pin that says, 'If I've known you in a previous life, please identify yourself'!"

Retirement also allowed June to fulfill a lifelong dream: she turned a room on the main floor of her house into a painting studio.

"I didn't paint before I retired because I had a big family and I worked," says June as she begins working on the small canvas lying in front of her. "I'd always played around with it but I never had time to paint. You don't get much time to paint and it's upsetting to everyone else in the house because it's a mess. You need your own space."

Out of her nine living children, thirteen grandchildren, and fifteen great-grandchildren, only one daughter and one granddaughter paint—none of her children became teachers. Although she has taken a few courses here and there (there being Alberta, where four children live), June is a self-taught painter and believes her artistic ability is built-in.

"I've always been able to draw. If I was making up a grocery list, the kids would make fun of me because there would be drawings all over it. If I was taking a course at school that was boring, there would be drawings all around my paper. Way back, I used to draw for my mother to make hooked mats. I'd draw flower arrangements and landscapes on the burlap."

Once she moved onto canvas, she joined the local painting group and now participates in the annual Mixed Palette Art Show and Sale, held at the end of July. Her paintings sell quite well.

"I started out with watercolours but I didn't hang with it long enough to get any control," explains June. "I went to acrylics then to oils. I like oils. They're stinky and dirty and messy and they destroy your clothes, but I like them."

She paints just about everything—"seascapes are hard but landscapes are easy"—but likes animals best, and horses in particular. Her favourite painting, which she refuses to sell, shows two deer leaping gracefully through snow. "I painted an eagle once and my grandson came over and said, 'It even looks like an eagle.' He was so shocked," she says with a chuckle.

Since she paints mainly from photographs and pictures in magazines, there are several spread around her end of the table. She's spent much of the morning working on a background.

"I don't think I'm good enough at mixing my colour to paint from my mind," she says. "Sometimes I mix something I shouldn't but it's getting much better. By the time I'm ninety-five, it'll be okay."

Although she's slowed down a bit and not painting every day, June rarely misses the once-a-week meetings of her painting group.

"If you don't get your Thursday painting, your week is off. And we don't gossip," she assures me, eyes twinkling. "Only intellectual conversation here."

8

Good Vibrations

Many years ago, when my father was a funeral director with his own business in Trenton, Ontario, two men and a young boy were killed when their personal aircraft crashed just after taking off from the lake in front of their family cottage.

On board were the pilot, his brother-in-law, and nephew. The pilot owned a Trenton car dealership, his brother-in-law was in the Armed Forces, and the boy was twelve. All of them were well known in our community, through jobs, school, church, and sports. Their deaths were sudden and tragic and shocking.

The visitation at our funeral home lasted hours past the allotted time, the line of mourners streaming out the front doors and along the sidewalk. There was one funeral for all three family members, with the father and son in the same casket, and attendance overflowed the largest church in town.

When my mother talks about my father's work and how he believed in the importance of public mourning, of taking time to grieve, pay respects, and share memories, she references this funeral. She talks about how challenging it was for my father because his business and community work intertwined with those of the deceased's. She remembers the staggering amount of people who came to the visitation and funeral, and how my father escorted both widows up the long, centre aisle of the church, one on either arm, his face grey with grief and strain. He, too, was a friend of this family, of these men and their wives. My father maintained his impeccable poise as a funeral director even though on this day, it wasn't business as usual. These deaths were personal and could not be held at a safe distance by professionalism or anonymity.

And that is as it should be.

I thought of this funeral and that familiar town one Monday morning as I sat down at my desk at the [now closed] community newspaper in Oxford, Nova Scotia, and tried to write the column I had planned for that week's issue. But the original idea wouldn't come; that file in my brain couldn't be accessed because two people from our small community had just died over the weekend. The circumstances of their deaths touched me even though I did not know them or their families personally.

Each of us knows the pain of death, whether sudden or expected, so when tragedy strikes, even outside our community, it resonates deeply. The horror of five sudden, terrible deaths—the halibut fishers aboard the *Miss Ally* who were lost at sea just two months prior—reverberated in our community even though we didn't know the young men personally. We shared the pain of their families and the communities of Cape Sable Island and Woods Harbour because we empathized.

The undeniable need for a different column that particular Monday came from the fact that two local women had died. This time it was personal for me, the come-from-away, the outsider, the journalist: my husband knew both families, and I recognized their names and the familial connections he explained.

The nature of their deaths influenced my need to write something else as well. One, a woman in her thirties, had died of complications following surgery; her death was unexpected, possibly avoidable, and she had a wide circle of friends. The other, a woman in her eighties, had lived a long, beloved life in which she experienced her own losses and joys. These would be two vastly different celebrations of life—one snuffed too soon, another full and complete—but both devastating losses to family and friends.

We do not remain untouched by the passing of a person, whether we know them or not. It is part of our human existence to mourn, to feel another's suffering, to share stories, and celebrate a life. Which is why, as I sat at my desk staring at my monitor and waiting for the right words, I thought about elephants.

My fascination with elephants began as I read Barbara Gowdy's 1998 novel, *White Bone.* Written from the perspective of elephants living on the plains of Africa, it certainly appealed to my interest in understanding the emotional and spiritual lives of animals. From that story, two important pieces of information had tucked themselves away in my brain and these ideas floated into my conscious mind on this morning, prompting me to research them further on the Internet.

Intelligent and social creatures, elephants mourn the same way humans do: with emotion and ritual. Those who study and work with elephants have witnessed familiar expressions of grief: elephants appear to cry and try to bury their dead. While experts say elephants don't fully understand the abstract concept of death, they do experience loss. They understand the deceased was once a part of the herd, part of the family, and is now gone. They don't walk away from their dead family member; they spend several days in mourning around the corpse.

Pachyderms also communicate with each other over remarkably long distances. The huge mammal has an exceptional ability to detect vibrations created through belly rumbles and foot stomps. Called "seismic communication," these vibrations are considered long-distance messages and can travel over a vast area—up to fifty kilometers—in order to reach other elephants, says a Stanford University biologist named Dr. Caitlin O'Connell-Rodwell

It seemed to me that receiving tragic news, processing, and reacting are all human vibrations. In a small community, whether we're talking one death or five, we operate the same way elephants do.

These vibrations make it possible for people to understand the circumstances, even if they have no connection to the person who has died. These vibrations, this shared knowledge, is what makes life in a small community so exceptional. Which is why, when I finally started to type, the thought that popped out of the jumble was, *the ideal place to die is in a rural area.*

It's not hyperbole. There are too many stories of people lying dead in their urban homes for days, no one missing them, to deny that what city dwellers consider nosiness—"I noticed your outside light is still on. Is everything alright?"—country people consider rallying around. It's a basic rule of engagement.

But the elephant-like vibration that rumbled me into awareness of these local deaths arrived in a most unexpected way about an hour before I left for work. Like so many others, I read the provincial obituaries every morning. I rarely know anyone, but I glance through the notices, allowing my attention be caught by an age, location, or long list of accomplishments. I read one particular obituary in its entirety because the woman had been from Oxford and was eighty-one. As I reached the last name on the list of those she left behind, I made the connection.

"Oh, no," I exclaimed, "Mr. Little's mom has died."

I hadn't recognized the woman's name but I knew her dog's. Even I, someone who doesn't live in town, recognized the pair. They were a common sight: the woman and her all-white Jack Russell terrier who trotted ahead of her, off-leash and perfectly behaved. For a moment, I experienced a sense of loss. I would miss seeing them, this woman and her delightful dog. Then came a second, underlying vibration: regret. Interviewing Mr. Little's human had been on my to-do list for ages, and I simply never got around to it.

As a come-from-away, I may not have a lifelong connection to this community but as a journalist, I have a reason to call someone up and talk. I meet a lot of people this way; I have often written stories about people who pass away weeks or months after our interview is published and I'm always glad I had the chance to share their stories: a tiny tone in the rumbling vibrations coursing through this small community.

In a rural area, if no one dies alone, it also means no one mourns alone. Death is life's great inevitable, so to pass on knowing your family, friends, and dog will be cared for, supported, and fed both physically and emotionally must be a comfort unique to small communities. It also means that when you phone eighty-year-old Grace to ask a question about the an upcoming potluck and the conversation moves onto the news, she will say to you, "Paul got away, eh?"

I can't think of a lovelier way to speak about the passing of a well-known man who was only sick for a short time. *He got away.*

With any death, the community will not let go—not before the funeral, and not after. The names of the deceased will be spoken widely, with kindness. There will be stories, memories, and while those who loved them will struggle with their absence, they will be spoken to and about with understanding. In fact, when it was publishing, our community newspaper devoted an entire page to personal notices expressing thanks for thoughtfulness shown during difficult times and remembering those who have passed on. Every so often, an "In Memoriam" was dedicated to someone who passed twenty years earlier.

Like a vibration passing through the community, a memory is stirred, a story is told, and a life lives on.

9

Check Me for Ticks

To say I've always had my hair cut in the city even if I live two hours away sounds like bragging but honestly: it's not. I blame this personal maintenance quirk on genetics (both my parents had thick, straight hair) and my mother's tendency to cart my sister and I to downtown Toronto every six weeks after a local stylist butchered my classic bowl cut. "It looks like it was cut with hedge trimmers," she said at the time.

Going to the city wasn't as snooty as it sounds. My mother was born in Toronto and her family still lived in and around the city. We would drive up the night before, stay at her sister's, then take the subway downtown. I have three distinct memories from those trips: The farmland that still surrounded Toronto; the excitement of riding the subway into the city centre; and shopping and eating lunch at the Eaton Centre after our hair appointments.

9

Going to a city salon is simply what I do. Some women spend their money on tans, tattoos, or acrylic nails; I spend mine on haircuts. I also like getting a city fix.

There are many things I miss about city life: living in a neighbourhood and walking to stores and restaurants. I miss the energy of all the people sitting in cafés, walking on streets, and browsing in stores. I miss the convenience and the variety of city living including sidewalks and streetlights. I love living in the country more, I just need a city fix every so often.

I'd lived in rural Nova Scotia for more than a year before I spent a couple of days tromping around Halifax. My husband was on a work-related course in the middle of May, so we stayed overnight and I had forty-eight glorious hours to scratch an itch that had been tickling for a while.

I spent a few hours at the Art Gallery of Nova Scotia, enjoyed a lunch of butternut squash soup and crab cakes, met my husband after his course, and sat on a patio drinking beer. I bought a sundress at a vintage clothing store, and obscure books of poetry at a used bookstore. Shopping until my feet swelled reminded me why I had come to prefer walking through the woods to walking on concrete. On day two, when my feet finally gave out at three o'clock in the afternoon, I went into Annie's Café on Birmingham Street and the woman behind the counter took one look at my face and asked, "What do you need, dear?"

Over the following few years, I remembered this two-day exploration of Halifax with such fondness, I knew there was a part of me that would always need a city fix, no matter how many chickens we kept or how many pairs of Bog boots I owned. So a couple of years later when I wanted to find a stylist in the city, the two-hour drive and twelve-dollar parking didn't deter me. This city trip had another upside: my mother was coming with me. Just like the good ol' days. (As in, she would buy lunch and take me shopping.)

Here's the thing about leaving the country to spend a day in the city: you feel a bit like a hayseed. Or rather, I do. Not my husband: he goes into the city wearing his camouflage coat and Western boots and doesn't give a flying fart what some city person might think. More accurately, he goes to Halifax dressed like that and no one cares because that's the joy of Halifax—there are more people with country roots in the city than there are city folk.

When I moved permanently to Nova Scotia at the end of March 2007, I kept busy for the first week or so unpacking and organizing and rearranging. Finally, I had to "go to town" and stopped by my husband's office at the local Department of Transportation garage to see if he needed anything.

"Well, look at you!" he said. "All fancied up for a trip to Amherst."

I was wearing eye shadow and a nice jacket.

And that's all I require for a trip to Halifax. There's no demand for "high fashion," no sense that you really have to dress up to not stand out. There isn't the same pressure one (me) feels when one (me) goes to Toronto, which I think we all agree—in the nicest possible way—is a completely different planet. Once you've moved to the Maritimes, you start to believe Toronto is actually a completely different solar system—also in the nicest possible way.

For my trip to Halifax with my mother, I simply put on my nicest clothes, just like in the olden days when farmers and their wives would trade work clothes for their Sunday best to take an infrequent trip to town. I just wanted to look a little less like a hayseed and a little more like a sophisticated grown-up. Don't judge me.

It was easy enough to choose a salon from the internet and make an appointment over the phone. It was easy enough to drive downtown and find a parking garage. But inside the salon was a whole other story: the familiar smells of shampoo, flattening irons, colour chemicals, and spray products all swirled in the moist, warm air. Snippets of conversation floated above the roar of hair dryers. The adult city girl inside me rose to the surface, nose in the air (sniffing, not snooting) while the adult country girl hid behind her, peering down at her footwear to makes sure she had worn the right kind of boots (leather, not rubber). Fortunately, my stylist, a young woman named Jessica, was completely unperturbed by her new client from the country.

Twenty years ago, I would have been self-conscious about being a hayseed in the city. I thought I knew everything about the world—and myself—and I just wanted to get out of my town as quickly as possible. When I ended up living in a condo in Vancouver with its soundtrack of sirens and view of other condos, I started to fantasize about a house in the country. On the opposite coast, of course: the west coast is gorgeous but it turns out the scraggy, scrappy east coast is where my heart longed to be.

When you're a hayseed at heart, it's only a matter of time before you end up living on a rural route with a coop full of chickens and your very own .22 in the gun cabinet.

"I didn't know you couldn't hunt on Sundays," Jessica said during one of my early appointments a few years ago.

I laughed. "Why *would* you know that?"

She snipped for a bit then said, "I can't wait to go out with my friends and tell them that."

This is how Jessica earned her tip: her interest in my stories about rural life was genuine. She listened to my descriptions of the unique personalities of each of our chickens. She expressed sympathy when I told her about Betty, our pet chicken, who was eaten by a fox. When I brought her half a dozen eggs, not only did she not blink when I told her there were only six because half the flock was moulting and therefore not laying, but the two green-shelled eggs intrigued her.

"I can't believe you don't have to put these in the fridge," she said after I'd explained she didn't have to worry about them while she worked. (As long as they're unwashed, farm-fresh eggs are naturally protected by their own coating and don't require refrigeration.)

Within a year, Jessica was an expert—at least, within her circle of city friends—on all things country. Before I sat down in her seat, Jessica didn't know nuthin' 'bout country livin'. For a girl who was born and raised in Halifax and worked at a downtown salon, she certainly looked and smelled like a city girl. But bless her concrete and asphalt heart, she didn't laugh at her new client who talked about chickens laying green-shelled eggs, learning to shoot a gun, and working at a weekly community newspaper. Although, now that I think about it, she might have checked me for ticks.

Now wouldn't the discovery of one of *those* set the fox amid the chickens? Who would have howled louder: the city girl who only has to deal with worms on the sidewalk after it rains, or the wannabe country girl who is secretly terrified of ticks?

"If you write a column about this, will you send it to me, please?" Jessica asked. "I'd love for my parents to read it."

"You'll be famous in Cumberland County," I told her.

It's nice, you know, when you can educate city people and help at least one city girl get in touch with her inner hayseed...if only to impress her friends.

10

It'll be All Right

When the red curtain of the Capitol Theatre in Moncton opens, Christina Martin stands centre stage, guitar strapped around her shoulders, big smile ready. This is the first of two Maritime concerts launching her latest CD. She's going with a new sound, adding a band and ramping up from country-folk-alternative to rock and roll. She looks amazing, sexy, and glamourous—she looks like a rock star. But I know a secret: Christina has an inner country girl.

Something else you may not know about this award-winning east coast musician who tours Canada and Europe: she is my neighbour. She lives around the country-corner from me. In publicity photos for her 2012 album, *Sleeping With a Stranger*, she's wearing a diaphanous dress and shawl and standing in front of a massive pile of cut logs. Trees that once stood between her house and mine. No matter where she travels, how glamourous her album covers, or how rock and roll her sound, her heart and home are in rural Nova Scotia.

I met Christina in 2012 after mutual acquaintances suggested I interview her; she was a vocal and creative supporter of mental health and people diagnosed with dementia. I called her up and asked if I could write a story about her and she said, "Great!"

When I arrived at her address on Carrington Road, the old wooden door to the green farmhouse was open, letting the bright March sunshine splash onto the floor inside. As I raised my hand to knock on the storm door, what I heard wasn't a drum roll or guitar riff, but unmelodious clattering.

"Come in," Christina said with a smile and a wave. "I'm making coffee. Would you like some?" She opened her china cabinet. "Choose your cup and saucer," she instructed. "These belonged to my grandmother."

As Christina puttered in the kitchen, I said hello to her producer-slash-husband, Dale, who was working in the next room, and looked around her home. The dining room window revealed a sweeping vista across fields and woods to the Northumberland Strait. The lovely antique dining room table matched the china cabinet. When we sat down at the table, she placed two lovely bone-china cups and saucers in front of us.

This is not how one pictures a professional musician living, all fine china and tidy farmhouse. Firstly, you'd think she would have to live in a city. Secondly, Christina's music is not strictly country or folk in the kitchen-party sense, and yet the qualities represented by those genres—the open spaces, the friendly people, the authentic storytelling—are what drew her away from the city in the first place.

"I'd been living in Halifax and Dale and I had been together for about seven years when we decided we wanted to move outside the city," Christina told me during that interview. "I love city life but I also had this dream of living somewhere peaceful and calm, without all the noise and distraction. We play a lot of rural areas. I've always loved playing in small, intimate, lovely places. I'm drawn to those areas."

Like me, Christina's childhood influence is urban, not rural; she was born in Fort Walton Beach, along the Florida panhandle, and as a child she lived in Fredericton, Rothesay, and Grand Falls, New Brunswick. She recorded her first album in Austin, Texas, before moving to Halifax where she studied business and psychology at university. But at her concerts she always mentions that she was raised in New Brunswick, upholding that quintessential Maritime tradition of establishing her rightful place in the east coast family tree.

She also married a man born and raised just down Route 6 in Pugwash, where his parents still live. When Christina and Dale were getting ready to move out of the city, his mother found them a place to rent on Wallace Bay. It soon became clear that if they wanted to fulfill their plan of working in the country, they would need a studio. Both Dale and Christina are musicians (Dale had released his first solo album the day before my visit) and he also is an award-winning producer.

"Someone was talking about this old farmhouse and I said, 'Can we go see it?' There were a few selling points," explained Christina about the large, three-bedroom house they moved into in January—January!—2011. "It was in great shape and it was perfect for what we needed. This whole place just radiated *Work, create, be at peace here* and I need that. I never dreamed we'd be in this kind of space this soon in our lives."

The move inspired the song and album title *Sleeping With A Stranger*, which includes this verse: "Wouldn't it be nice to move away/Buy a little house down in Wallace Bay/A dream home with a hammock and fireplace/To lay our tired little bones?"

Christina paused to refill our teacups. Through the window, a garden plot lay in the promising disarray of early spring.

"Are you handy?" I asked her by way of wondering if she has time to garden.

"We're learning to be handy," Christina replied and I understood the many layers in her answer. When you move to the country, you quickly realize how much there is to do, and most of it you should—or think you should—do yourself. "I like to do things and if I had more time and money, I would be handier. I don't think Dale would be offended if I said he is not handy."

Behind us, from the room transformed into Dale's studio, came an emphatic, "No."

So they hired local help and learned people were quite happy to pitch in, as they hadn't expected these citified neighbours to know how to do anything.

"You kind of build a little family, you know, with the plumber and the electrician; those guys who come by more than you wished you needed them," Christina laughed. "We've had a lot of furnace guys coming in."

I wanted to know if the remote nature of their home and studio could be an obstacle.

"We knew we wanted it and it wasn't a false desire," said Christina. "We settled right in. It's really beautiful here. When we tour with a new album, we're on the road for about a year and a half so that's my social time, that's when I meet people. But I really value my time alone. I need that to be creative and to organize and do my work."

Amen, sister.

"There are benefits to being in the city," she admitted. "I love things about city life and there are more performance and promotion opportunities in a city...but not necessarily a financial benefit. We were lucky that we were at a point in our musical careers where we could afford to buy a house. Even though we have to drive two hours to Halifax or Moncton or wherever the gig is, it's still more affordable for us to be living and working here."

On the back of the CD cover for that 2012 album, written and recorded entirely in rural Nova Scotia, is a review by Bob Mersereau of CBC Fredericton which (in part) read: "For all of us trying to find the life we're meant to live, here's a soundtrack."

Three years later, as she struts around on stage at the Capitol Theatre, introducing a new look, new sound, and ten new songs to an audience of family, friends, and devoted fans, it's clear country living hasn't held Christina back: it has transformed her. She's adventurous, resilient, happy. She has a family of musicians around her helping with this new artistic journey; a journey that stems from a special place overlooking fields, water, woods, and gravel roads. A place to work, create, and be at peace. A place in the country.

11

A Hot Time in the Old Town

————··————

There are three traditional east coast talents I wish I possessed: rug hooking, jig dancing, and fiddle playing. Since my early exposure to rural Nova Scotia was limited to two weeks every summer and didn't involve music or crafts, the opportunity to learn never presented itself.

Perhaps if I hadn't become a permanent resident on a rural route and my ever-widening circle of acquaintances hadn't included rug hookers, songwriters, painters, and guitar players, I might not have realized I lacked these talents. I might not have felt cheated out of truly experiencing the heart of Maritime country life. The sad truth is I will probably never experience a genuine kitchen party—not in its purest, most original form.

Sure, my family once organized a Saturday night kitchen party at our summer home on Pugwash Point, but we had to hire musicians and issue invitations so it lacked true spontaneity. Until it closed in the spring of 2016, the café in Pugwash hosted a "Friday Night Kitchen Party" throughout the summer months, while at biweekly "jam sessions" in Oxford, local musicians play to a full house. But what I think of as a real, honest-to-goodness kitchen party happens spontaneously—yet regularly—in an actual kitchen. It includes people who always have a fiddle or banjo at the ready or a harmonica in their pocket. People who don't have to be cajoled into taking part, who pick up their instruments without being asked and don't use sheet music. Then, into that mix of notes, someone jumps up and begins to move her feet. A partner joins her and suddenly, the Hoosier cabinet begins to rattle, beer bottles tumble off the table, and someone yells about wasting good water.

At least, that's what I imagine a Maritime kitchen party looks and sounds like. Do they exist anymore or are kitchen parties, like bales of hay and skating parties on a pond, one more traditional rural activity drifting away on the tides of memory?

I sometimes wonder if this hankering is from a previous life when I might have been a Cape Breton fiddler...there's just something about fiddle music that makes my heart sing. Put me in a symphony hall with a dozens of violins and my heart recoils; I yearn for the fling of a fiddle, not the whine of a violin.

I grew up with a mother who played piano, sang, and conducted a couple of church choirs. While my younger sister followed in her footsteps, I gave up piano lessons when I was fourteen because I don't possess that inherent sense of rhythm necessary for spontaneous playing and dancing. Mostly, though, kitchen parties were not tradition in Ontario—not as a province and not as a family. There were evenings my mother would invite friends from church over to play, and I only remember the name of the man who brought his fiddle (Clary Page), no one else. I listened from the top of the stairs, dressed in my pyjamas, and leaning against the wall instead of lying in bed asleep. Did children in Nova Scotia get to stay downstairs for the music only to fall asleep in someone's lap, lulled by the rhythm of a leg bouncing in time to the fiddlers?

(It just occurred to me that true love really is blind: I didn't marry a Nova Scotia country boy who plays the fiddle. At least my husband wishes he played an instrument as much as I wish I knew how to jig.)

Despite the adult-onset regret that I didn't keep at the piano lessons, I know I wouldn't feel this lack so keenly if such amazing talent didn't surround me. It's almost masochistic to attend these café kitchen parties and jam sessions. As our rural populations decline, as schools drop art and music classes, these "open mic" music nights held in community and church halls, small cafés, and old theatres need our support more than ever.

If you're missing them, you're missing out: the talent that shows up is astonishing. As my husband regularly says as we drive home from most nights of live music, "Bar none, that was the best night of music we've ever heard." Each week seems to top the week before. The performances, especially from teenagers, actually take our breath away—and not just from singing along.

These home-grown performers don't make any money; they come out to their preferred venue simply for the love of playing, for the thrill of getting up in front of friends and strangers, and for the satisfaction of doing something they enjoy. The crowd, often filled with supporters like my husband and me who possess no musical talent, becomes increasingly envious—and regretful—as the night goes on.

One evening at the café in Pugwash, two brothers, still in high school, came to sing and play their guitars. The younger brother had a tough time hitting a high note, and got embarrassed. He hesitated, as if to walk away, but the crowd wouldn't let him: we encouraged him to start again, and when he nailed that note on the second try, our claps and cheers almost drowned him out.

In front of a crowd, once the first song is over and the blast of nerves passes, young performers visibly relax, open up, and grow more confident right before our eyes. One weekend, a seventeen-year-old boy visiting from Cape Breton wowed the small audience with his guitar and vocal skills. Afterwards, a seasoned veteran of performing encouraged him to "keep at it." Hopefully, that's all the young musician needed to hear to keep nurturing his talent.

For almost a decade the Main Street Music Society at Oxford's historical Capitol Theatre has welcomed seasoned—and terrified—performers during its biweekly Friday Night Jam. The society's chairperson, Eleanor Crowley, estimated that half of the performers are playing or singing in public for the first time.

"If you have the nerve or the desire, you can get up on the stage. It's a good place to start if you're musically inclined and want to do more with it. And it's family, friends, and neighbours in the audience. We'll clap for you. Sometimes it might be because you got down," she laughs, "and sometimes it might be because you got up, but we clap regardless."

She told me about one woman who was an excellent singer but had terrible stage fright; this venue gave her the courage to try, and eventually she got past her fear and became a solid performer. One man, who had attended the early sessions, just happened to show up at the fifth anniversary jam. According to Eleanor, his transformation was remarkable.

"He got up on stage again and the change in him from when we started—he was an actual performer. It's amazing to watch the evolution," said Eleanor. "You can tell [first-timers] because they're not used to using the mic; they'll pick and play with their head down, almost as if they're singing to themselves."

The musicians and crowds at the Oxford jam nights tend to be older, playing and appreciating country and bluegrass music. Eleanor only gets up on stage to emcee and says even though she didn't grow up in a musical family, she remembers hanging around musical people: "Kitchen parties would just spring out of nothing. So-and-so would land, and there was always a guitar sitting around somewhere. Someone would bring theirs in from the car. Somebody always had a guitar in the car," she laughed. "You'd go for a drive and park somewhere and someone would play and everyone in the car would sing."

How many generations have passed their evenings singing and playing instruments in their own homes, music and laughter the soundtrack for the night? How many teenagers, when handed a harmonica, fiddle, or guitar, learned to play surrounded by mentors?

Now that ear buds and smart phones provide distraction and demand attention, could we be raising a generation that doesn't know the thrill and inspiration of a spontaneous jam session? Those moments are a testament to the quality of talent and the joy of musical communion; everyone goes home with a song in their hearts and a promise to keep it there.

What Eleanor said about musical instruments lying around and giving children their start reminds me of another childhood musical experience. Back in the early eighties, family friends had given us a hand-me-down, kid-sized drum set. My sister and I recruited our two best friends and created a band called "The Goldenrods." We wrote one song. Our captive audience was our four parents, who graciously listened to our concert in a cottage with no ceiling or insulation, just open rafters and a peaked roof. Imagine the acoustics. And since the cottage was open-concept, technically we could consider our one and only performance a spontaneous kitchen party.

We were ten years old—and *bad*—but thirty years later, my sister still remembers the lyrics to that song. That's what music—the home-grown, kitchen party kind—is meant to do: leave a lasting impression on your heart.

The Country Lives
of Animals

1

City Dog, Country Dog

When I moved to Nova Scotia in 2007, I came with boxes of books, suitcases of clothes, and a four-year-old boxer named Stella. Having spent four summers running around the fields and beaches of Pugwash Point and four winters escaping the confines of a townhouse by tramping the fields and woods of a family friend's farm in Ontario, Stella was ready to embrace the freedom of permanent residency in the country.

The country convenience of simply opening the door and letting the dog out—without having to leash her and take her for a walk every time—allowed Stella to pursue one of her greatest pleasures: wandering around by herself and doing her own thing, which was, I'm afraid, searching for poop to eat—deer, rabbit, even cow. She quickly learned the boundaries of the two-acre yard but also that out back, there were no boundaries and seventy more acres of unlimited sniffing and snacking delight.

About a week after we had arrived and settled in, Stella dragged home the long, clean spine of an animal. That was how Dwayne learned the first lesson of living with Stella: don't bait coyotes with beaver carcasses because Stella will find them. Every time. No matter where they are.

Within a few years, it occurred to me that, with all the space around us, there was plenty of room for another dog. I could picture it perfectly: walking through the fields and woods with two dogs playing and running ahead of me. My imaginings neglected to picture Stella disappearing into the woods, lagging behind me to eat deer poop, and generally never, ever coming when I called. Nor did it include the dog throwing up whatever rotten thing she'd found and eaten at three o'clock in the morning.

"Can we get a puppy?" I asked my husband every six months.

"No," he always answered.

"But we have seventy-two acres. There's lots of room for another dog."

"There's seventy-two acres out there, but the house is only forty-two feet long and that's where the dogs will be all the time," he countered.

His clever rejoinder made me want to bite him.

The alpha male of our household finally accepted the inevitability of getting another dog when my friend Jane got a puppy at the end of June. So when I came home from work one evening in early October and announced I had found a litter of boxer puppies in Stellarton that would be ready to go in November, he didn't flinch. He didn't even glare when I informed him we were going to visit the one available female pup that very Saturday.

Saturday rolled around and we found ourselves sitting on the floor in the back room of a pet supply store: one of the store's owners had the boxer puppies while the other had Bernese mountain dog puppies. A lone pug seemed to think he was in charge of them all. While I defended myself from a fluffy Bernese attack, a dark brown boxer puppy crawled onto my husband's lap.

"Which puppy is the available female?" he asked as he petted the pup.

"The one in your lap."

Well, now, as signs go, they don't get much clearer than that.

So just as the November cold swept in, accompanied by wind and snow, we brought home our new puppy, Abby, and introduced her to eight-year-old Stella.

I didn't know what to expect from Stella—she'd had an older sister herself when she was a pup—but I didn't expect complete tolerance. She put up with not only the constant biting and demands to play, but also the sharing of bones (!) and total invasion of her personal space. Wherever Stella lay, the pup was on her like a remora stuck to a shark.

This calm and accepting Stella took some getting used to because my memories of her as a younger dog remained vivid. Like a recurring nightmare, in fact.

When she was a puppy, Stella's nickname was "Frankenstella" because she was such a little monster. Back in Ontario, I once chased her around our neighbourhood because she'd run off with a banana I'd set on the doorstep while I retied my shoelaces. I was also going through a divorce so it's likely the anger and anxiety she sensed in me made her overly protective, which in turn made her aggressive towards other dogs. On the other hand, she loved people and had this awful habit of spying someone in the distance and dragging me down the sidewalk to greet them. Shortly before we moved to Nova Scotia, a neighbour said to me, "We're going to miss you. Watching you try and train your dog has kept us entertained these past four years."

"You know, Stell," I said to her as we fetched the newspaper one morning while the puppy chased after a blowing leaf, "the upside of all this chaos and constant trips outside for peeing is that I now have a deeper appreciation for you."

Six months after the puppy arrived, I mentioned obedience classes to my husband and he looked at me like I had two heads.

"Why would you want to spend money on obedience classes?" he asked, incredulous.

That's when the city girl and the country boy locked horns. To him, training a puppy meant putting her outside, letting her figure things out as she goes, and yelling at her when she does something you don't like. For me, a dog must understand half a dozen basic commands or cues, and the best way to make sure you are doing it correctly is to attend weekly classes. Stella did; she even graduated although she seemed to believe "Come, Stella," applied only when we were in class.

Since obedience *can* be taught without a class, my greatest motivation for taking the puppy to class was to socialize her. It's one thing to teach her to be a country dog—to go snowshoeing, ride on the four-wheeler, not chase the chickens, and not venture past the mailbox—but it's another thing to take her into the city. There, she would experience a multitude of sounds, smells, and activity.

When I thought about it, I'd spent more than ten years walking Stella in busy urban areas so I was hard-wired—and a bit desperate—for this new dog to be relaxed and have good manners. A well-behaved country dog must know it can never, *ever* jump up on the side of a vehicle—several long, deep toenail scratches down the driver-side door of a brand new truck is the kind of thing that can put a friendship in the doghouse.

I made a lot of mistakes training Stella, the big one being a lack of consistency. One of the best pieces of advice I ever received when Stella was already set in her ways was, "start as you mean to go on." Obedience classes with Abby were my way of preventing bad behaviour from developing. (That advice applies to most aspects of life, not just puppy training; it was especially pertinent after I'd married a set-in-his-ways country boy.)

My friend Jane wanted to know if the classes were about socialization or training.

"Both," I told her. "We'll both be trained and socialized."

I could hate her for this because perfect dogs are the bane of my existence, but Jane's puppy, Sam, did not need obedience classes. Apparently, he was born fully trained because he walked perfectly off the leash from six months of age, is never aggressive with other dogs, and comes when he is called.

Almost immediately—as if I need any further reminders that I am utterly lacking the right energy for dog training—I recognized the vibe Jane gives off. It says, "I'm in charge here. Yes, you're adorable, but don't mess with me." Dogs not only respond to that energy, they respect it. The only reason I get any attention from a dog is my pocket full of peanut butter treats.

I love dogs, I want to have them as companions, and I often prefer their company to people, but my energy encourages dogs to walk all over me. My confidence needs constant boosting and rebooting, and I get that from people who have a natural affinity for working with dogs. They remind me that every moment with a dog is a training moment. Jane says if you only teach your dog one command, make it the recall one; a dog that comes when it is called, freezes when it hears its name, or returns to you immediately when it hears the word "come," is going to be safer, happier, and more trustworthy (and more full of treats). I have to admit I've kind of given up on the dream of living with a dog that comes when she's called.

But Jane reminded me that taking my dogs for walks in woods around my home makes recall particularly essential. I'm supposed to stop thinking about column topics while the dogs run wild and instead, recognize every moment as a training moment.

Hmmm? Were you saying something? I was thinking about how to write about this for my next column.

This wandering attention habit was something I picked up almost immediately upon moving to the country with Stella. After the hyper-vigilance required for walking her in the city, it was such a luxury to relax and just let her wander. When I walk the trails around our property, I crave peace and quiet. I set my brain to autopilot, and I don't want to pay attention to anything but the path under my feet and the birds in the trees. If that means allowing the dogs to wander off and be free of my nagging commands for a while, however naive that may be, I'm fine with it.

In only one way did Stella fail to completely embrace country living: we were never able to teach Stella how to ride on a four-wheeler. Dwayne could get her to jump up on the back seat, but as soon as he started moving, Stella would jump off. Fearing she would break a leg, we gave up. At sixty pounds, she was too heavy to ride on my lap, so Stella had to stay home. The problem was she wanted to be with us. One autumn afternoon, I happened to look back as we struck out along the unimproved road that runs alongside our land, and saw Stella running behind, trying to keep up. She was no longer used to that kind of endurance running but I was familiar with her big-heartedness. She would try to follow me even if it killed her.

With the new puppy, we commenced four-wheeler training right away. We were pleased to have a canine companion as we headed deep into the woods on a winter's afternoon. When we stopped at the Ducks Unlimited pond to snowshoe across its frozen surface, the energetic puppy scampered along behind.

Start as you mean to go on.

2

The Blessing of the Ospreys

In the late 1980s, my husband put up a tall pole with a large steel wheel nailed to the top on the far edge of his rural property. The pole had a view of the River Philip, and he hoped (in vain) it would attract a pair of eagles. For thirty years, the wheel remained vacant and ignored.

After we married in the summer of 2007, we spent our first year together fixing up the house and yard he'd been neglecting since his first marriage had ended five years earlier. I painted the walls and he installed new windows; he built decks and I dug flower gardens. We built a chicken coop and filled it with a flock. The property blossomed with our new partnership.

"I've never seen the lilacs come out so full," Dwayne said the first spring after our wedding.

"The trees and plants must sense a new energy here now," I answered. I'd learned, through many dog obedience classes, that a human's energy affects the dog at her side: if she is calm, the dog is calm; if she is angry or fearful, the dog will sense that and become agitated or even aggressive. Since I was already predisposed to believe human energy could affect animal energy, I was quite ready to believe true love between two humans could affect the growing potential of the plants around them. But what happened later that summer proved the theory applied beyond pets and plants.

On July first, a month before our first wedding anniversary, my husband raised a hand to shade his eyes as he looked across the yard.

"Look!" he exclaimed. "Look what's flying around the pole!"

As I looked up from my weeding, two ospreys landed on the wheel. They spent most of the day there, circling, landing, flying off, and returning. They kept coming throughout the following weeks, often clutching sticks in their talons. Slowly, the two birds laid the foundation for a nest.

Ospreys are also known as "fish hawks" since their diet consists only of fish. This pair had found prime real estate along the river, which is full of sea trout, gaspereau, and striped bass. As fish eaters, they posed no threat to our chickens wandering around the coop a mere hundred metres from their nest. In fact, the ospreys showed no sign of fear—or annoyance—at our proximity to their new home. It appeared they were willing neighbours.

Part of the raptor family, ospreys have a wingspan of almost two metres and weigh just shy of five pounds. Because fish makes up 99 percent of their diet, they typically nest along rivers, lakes, and coastlines. They also return to the same nest every year.

"The osprey haven't been here in a couple of days," Dwayne commented one late-August evening as we watered our gardens.

We looked up at the wheel covered in a smattering of branches and wondered if we'd see them again.

Over the winter, I investigated the sudden arrival of the ospreys: I had bought Ted Andrews's book, *Animal Speak: The Spiritual and Magical Powers of Creatures Great and Small,* at a yard sale. In the book, Andrews, who taught shamanic principles and claimed to be a clairvoyant, discusses birds and animals as symbols and spirit guides; it seemed an appropriate tome to own now that I lived in the country. According to the book, which sold more than five hundred thousand copies between 1993 and 2009, an osprey is a symbol of vision and guardianship. "Hawks are messengers, the protectors, the visionaries of the air," Andrews writes. "This power bird can awaken power and lead you to your life's purpose. It is the messenger bird, and wherever it shows up, pay attention. There is a message coming."

I wondered what the message from that pair of ospreys was. I'd begun to wonder if it was meant for me. It's one thing to marry for love, to leave family and friends to join your soulmate in a completely different life, even if it was the kind of life for which you'd been yearning. It's another thing to discover purpose to that life.

Being a writer and feeling ambivalent about teaching (particularly since most of the available work was substituting) meant I was starting to feel adrift in this new life. The ospreys arrived at this long-vacant platform just as I was wondering if I could find meaningful work outside the house, beyond the gardens and chickens. I couldn't help but take this sudden arrival of "messenger hawks" personally.

The following spring, on a sunny and cool Sunday afternoon in mid-April, we were cleaning up the yard when I heard my husband shout from across the yard where he was raking old, wet leaves: "Honey, look! The ospreys are back!"

I straightened up and looked over at the nest. Sure enough, an osprey was sitting on the edge of the bit of nest that survived the winter. As I watched, a second one flew into sight, circling the nest a couple of times before swooping in to land next to its mate. We had no way of confirming if it was the same pair who had started building the nest the year before so we chose to assume it was.

"It's so great they came back," Dwayne said with a happy grin.

The ospreys continued to build up the nest, one bird always remaining inside. It was early July when we saw a small head pop up above the edge of the nest. Our ospreys, as we quickly came to consider them, had hatched a baby.

By early September, all three birds had left the nest. I stood at the edge of our property one evening, orange sunset blazing in the sky, and stared up at the silhouette of the nest. Now began the long wait for their spring return. Now began our annual worry about whether they would return or not.

Ospreys are snowbirds. They leave their summer habitat—which can be as far north as Labrador—in the early fall and fly as far south as the Caribbean. They are one of the most widespread birds of prey and can be found on every continent except Antarctica. All that mattered to us, however, was that they made a safe return "home" from their journey down south.

The "Summer of the Osprey" began with a mid-April return, a few weeks of rebuilding the nest ravaged by the winter winds, and then the long sit on the eggs. In early June, Dwayne had surgery on his right foot and his recuperation would take all summer. For a man used to working all the time, it was not easy for him to sit on the front deck and watch the world go by.

Until one of the ospreys took notice.

"I swear it's looking right at me when it flies over," Dwayne said to me one evening as we sat on the front deck in the warm summer air. Indeed, as the bird took a low swoop over our house, we could clearly see bright yellow eyes—the same eyes that can spot a fish from as high as thirty metres. On its way back to the nest to feed the sitting female, the male osprey often flew over the house carrying a large fish.

"Drop it here," Dwayne would holler from his deck chair, holding his hands up. "Drop that fish right here!"

In order to watch the nest itself, Dwayne began sitting on the back deck, positioning his chair for the perfect sightline between the two birch trees behind the house. The osprey nest was only five hundred metres from the house; close enough to see clearly, far enough away to avoid disturbing them.

On July 5, Dwayne hobbled into the house as fast as he could. "There's a baby in the nest," he told me, grabbing the binoculars.

It was the first sighting of that year's offspring. Within a week, there were three hatchlings. We took it as a sign that the birds knew they were welcome and felt safe enough to produce their full complement of babies.

Dwayne, his foot heavily bandaged, spent the rest of the summer on the back deck watching the ospreys raise their babies. He watched as one adult flew in to drop off a fish then take off again. He learned which high, piercing call meant a fish was coming in, and which set of rapid cries meant the fish had arrived. He watched the young ones grow bigger and stronger. He watched them stretch their wings and hop from one side of the nest to the other. He watched one chick, the largest and likely first-hatched, take its first breathtaking leap from the nest.

"This is so amazing," Dwayne would marvel several times a day. Always referring to them as "our ospreys," these birds became more than neighbours; they became part of our family. Every time we stepped out the back door or pulled into the driveway, our eyes sought the nest and the familiar silhouette of an osprey. Every morning, as I walked across the yard to release the chickens into their outside pen, I'd glance at the nest and murmur, "Good morning, ospreys."

We took great satisfaction in watching them soar over the house and hearing them chirp as they swooped low. *Surely this behaviour isn't normal*, I thought, *surely they're showing an unusual interest in us*. They had to be telling us something.

I believed the good energy emanating from our property attracted this pair; they were a couple and were building a home together— just like Dwayne and me. After twenty-five years, two houses were being transformed into homes. Perhaps their message was simple: build for the future but enjoy each day as it comes.

As a chronic worrier, that was a message I needed to hear. Part of being human means we like knowing what the future holds—we want to make long-term plans and exert control—yet all nature knows is uncertainty. Too much rain keeps bees from pollinating, or a cowbird lays an egg in a sparrow's nest, crowding out her smaller babies. Dwayne and I could never know if the ospreys flying away in the fall would return the following spring; their first year is the hardest and a lack of hunting experience coupled with the long migration could be a death sentence.

By mid-September, all five ospreys had left the nest and Dwayne returned to work. The Summer of the Osprey was over.

But that's not where the story, or the message, ends.

The following summer, we renovated our house and put on an addition for my mother. Since my father had died two years earlier, my mother had sold their summer house on Pugwash Point in order to live with us. "I'd like to bury your father's ashes on your property," she said and we all knew the perfect spot: under the osprey nest. My father, born and raised in southern Ontario, revelled in every sighting of an eagle or an osprey when he was on vacation in Nova Scotia.

Dwayne had a friend with a backhoe clear and build up a space—which we now call The Mound—and then held a brief ceremony. We interred the ashes along with my father's favourite driver (Dad was a golfer), a cup of Tim Hortons coffee with one cream (his favourite beverage and one he recognized even deep inside dementia), and a small bottle of his favourite whiskey (Crown Royal). We buried him with the ashes of his cats (Percy and Pickens) and dog (Lisa), the four of them together under a Colorado blue spruce—the same kind of tree that had grown in front of the first funeral home he'd ever owned.

In the weeks following the little ceremony, I built a stone bench near the tree so we could sit on The Mound under the osprey nest. When the bench was finished, I sat down on it, talked to my father, and had a good cry. I heard the familiar call of our favourite birds and looked up—way up.

There was no incoming bird and no fish delivery: just three young ospreys, all sitting on the edge of the nest, staring down at me with the bright orange eyes of fledglings. It seemed as if, through these ospreys, with their nodding heads, intense gazes, faithful return each spring, and swooping gestures over our home, my father was sending a message that he approved of the way we were building for the future.

3

Communion with the Livestock

○————•••————○

Walking along a rural road is a different experience than walking down a city street. I've traded sidewalks, parks, traffic lights, and house-lined streets for a gravel shoulder, fields, and trees, and every so often, a mailbox and a house. In the city I could walk for hours, day or night, and take a different route every time.

My new walking route goes to Carrington Road where Stella and I turn around and head back home. That narrow loop takes an hour, and we walk it early in the morning in the spring, summer, and early fall. I miss sidewalks and streetlights only because their absence limits the times of day we can walk.

We have become familiar to drivers heading to and from work, particularly my husband's co-workers at the Department of Transportation, or the shift workers heading to or from the salt mine in Pugwash. In early spring and fall, when we walk at seven because of the later sunrise, we get to wave to Debbie Field, the school bus driver.

This morning walk to Carrington Road and back takes us past three different herds of beef cattle. I know the milking cows by breed—Holsteins and Jerseys—but the beef cattle are identifiable only by colour: the black ones, the brown ones, the brown-and-white ones. But I don't need to know their breed to say good morning.

It's my first spring in rural Nova Scotia. The cows in the pasture next door are the first ones to greet Stella and I as we set out on our walk down the road. In the first few days of May, the cattle are finally released from the muddy yards around their barns into the soft, green fields. The young calves trot across the field towards us as if curious about the little brown "cow" walking alongside me.

After a month of life in the pasture, the calves relax and are only mildly interested in the human walking by with the funny brown cow on the leash. They already flick their tails and ears in the cow-like way of their mothers.

Farther along, past the white clapboard Presbyterian church, there is a lovely surprise across the road in the field with the abandoned house: a baby bull calf is standing on his crooked dark-brown legs. He's at least a day old, perhaps two, because he is not wobbly on those legs like a newborn. Mama is handy with milk, but a calf needs to learn to stand on its own immediately to keep up.

"Congratulations," I say to the cow. "That's a handsome son you have."

On the way back home, the older kids—the three May calves who are now twice the size of the newborn—are checking out the calf. In response, the little one is leaping around. If cows are able to express emotion, then this calf is doing happy: "Look at me! Born into this great big world with this soft green grass and the singing birds and all the milk I can drink! I am so happy!"

The bull, his broad, jowly face wrinkled and smudged with creamy hair, keeps his eye on the dog and me.

"A fine son you have," I tell him sincerely. From my summer vacations at the farm on Pugwash Point, I know it's wise to keep on the good side of a bull (and a fence).

Even I can tell this is a first-class bull calf; his coat is a rich dark brown and has no white markings at all. Reality intrudes on this spring morning: here is the birth of veal. I prefer to think that because he is so handsome, this bull calf will be sold as breeding stock.

Across the road in a smaller herd, I notice another new calf suckling its mother. The dog and I stand on the shoulder of the road for a long time, watching, listening, breathing. It's a beautiful sight. This is the quiet pleasure of a country morning.

My husband's uncle lost a calf the week before and had carted the corpse, in the loader of his tractor, past our house to dump it deep in the woods. This is the profoundness of nature I both dread and crave: life becomes death becomes earth becomes life. The death of any creature saddens me—there is now a mother cow searching for her baby—but there is always the joy of a brand-new calf gambolling in a field while its mother chews her cud and watches.

It's my first autumn in rural Nova Scotia. On our way home from Carrington Road, as we walk down the hill towards the church, a nicker carries through the cool air. I see a horse by the abandoned house, standing near a cow. The horse trots towards us, along the fence, her breath coming in pale puffs. As we reach her, she stands still at the fence, tall and lean, her brown coat shining in the early morning sun.

Stella prances at the end of the leash but doesn't seem to know what to do: should she bark or growl or simply sniff this strange and gorgeous beast? Overwhelmed by this new experience, the dog says nothing as we pass, an overgrown ditch and an electric fence between us. The horse nickers so I stop again and turn. The heavy, horned cow is trudging away and the horse gallops towards it. She then cuts a sharp right to come trotting, with a few leg kicks and hind bucks, back to the fence. She stops and remains unmoving and watchful. I tug the dog's leash and we walk on.

Crossing over the culvert that guides the creek under the road, we pass my father-in-law's field where the cattle also graze. This morning, I see no cows, which means they are grazing down by the river, out of sight behind the rolling hill. The sun's cool yellow rays, just now topping the thick bank of trees on the other side of the river, highlight the heavy dew on the meadow and create the hint of mist hovering over the grass.

I hear the horse we just passed neigh again, and I turn back to see her run into the gully, which is thick with trees. I wait, but she doesn't appear in this field. Just as I return to our walk, the dog now impatient for her breakfast, I hear hooves on earth and there she is, galloping across the open field. Her long legs propel her through the diamonds of dew, a drumbeat beneath her, while white clouds of breath trail behind her. Her coat glistens in the sun as she gallops—almost wild, almost free—across the wide pasture.

At the far end, she stops and whinnies. She stands for a moment, glorious in her power and energy, and gives me one last look before she disappears down to the river's edge.

In all the time we stand there and watch her, not a single vehicle drives by.

━◦•◦━

It's springtime, seven years later. Over time, the number of cows along my walking route dwindles. My father-in-law's field is no longer rented out for pasture and the brown horse disappears. I start a regular, part-time job that limits my morning walks to a few days a week. We get a puppy, and I start walking in town with my friend Jane and her puppy, Sam. Cows and calves and horses come and go, and we don't really notice the change in livestock as much anymore.

So I don't remember exactly when the miniature horses arrived or when I first met them. All I know is stopping to feed and pat them has become the sweet spot of my days.

It starts one morning in late May when the two horses happen to be in the field with the abandoned house. I stop to say hello. They take a few tentative steps towards us, me and the two dogs standing stiff and alert at the end of their leashes, but they don't come close. A few days later, I look ahead and see them in the field so I pick a handful of clover and hold it over the fence when we draw near. The brown mini walks over slowly and sniffs the proffered clover. She eats her share but won't get close enough for me to touch her nose. I toss the darker horse's share towards her and she eats it off the ground.

This becomes the routine: say hello, present a bunch of clover, and draw the miniature horses closer and closer until they allow me to pat them. The smaller, darker horse—who looks a bit like a hippopotamus—is less forward because the larger brown one nips at her and tries to hog the food. I sneak extra clover to the dark horse with the sweet hippo face.

Over time, the horses come to recognize us and seem to be waiting in that field each morning as if they've figured out the schedule. I stop for a visit and a snack on my way to Carrington Road and on the way back; I just can't walk past their faces looking at me expectantly from the other side of the road.

Throughout the summer, as the horses and I get to know each other, a large grey horse hovers in the periphery. Even if he is in the roadside field with the minis, he doesn't come over; he shows no interest in what is happening at the fence.

Not until I start offering apples in the fall.

Across the road from the field an old apple tree grows along the long driveway leading up to a house. Red apples scatter the ground so I scoop up several, crack them into pieces with the heel of my shoe, and offer them to the two horses.

The second time I do this, the old grey horse walks over as if he knows it's not merely clover I offer. I hold out my flattened hand with the apple slice on the palm, and his soft lips graze my skin. The third time, he trots over for an apple and allows me to touch his big, velvety nose. The bliss of that moment! The fourth time—and all the times that follow—he allows me to pat his face, his neck, his chest.

By now, you must sense how much this means to me, this touching, this interaction, this morning ritual. The miniature horses are small, their mouths and teeth manageable, but this giant horse is being gentle and sweet, letting me be his friend. My heart swells when the three of them see the three of us coming along the road and they trot alongside the fence to our meeting spot (an overgrown driveway blocked by the electric fence). They wait while I collect apples, and they nudge me for more when they're through munching. They are neither nippy nor skittish; the horses are happy to eat right from my hand.

This is not a weird thing to be thankful for. The horses are grateful for the apples, sure, but I am much more grateful for their acceptance of me, for their willingness to be fussed over by this city girl who has never had a horse of her own. If they sense I know nothing about horses, they don't hold it against me. Not as long as I'm offering apples.

"You were gone a long time this morning," my husband observes when I arrive home after more than an hour.

"I had a visit with my friends," I reply, and joy ripples through my body.

4

Rescue Me

They were dogs found in such horrific conditions or horrifying circumstances their stories made the news: The "mushkadoodles" flown in from Labrador. The "Preston puppies" rescued by an RCMP officer. The "garbage bag puppies" discovered in a ditch in Cape Breton. Their stories and photos shocked viewers but as the news cycled on, the behind-the-scenes account was never explored.

What did all these dogs have in common besides neglect and/ or abuse? They had all landed in the loving care of "Auntie Jane," a retired Cumberland County nurse known for her volunteer work with rescue dogs—work that wasn't even on her list of retirement plans.

Jane Jorgensen runs a grooming salon and boarding kennel in Wallace Bay on the family farm her husband, Gordon, took over from his father in the mid-seventies.

"We married in secret in 1977," she explains as she leads a freshly washed and dried golden retriever into a crate to await his owners. "I was still in nursing school in New Glasgow, and we weren't allowed to get married. It was the only training school in Canada that still had that rule. We had a church wedding and everything but every Sunday night, I took off my wedding ring and returned to school for another week."

It was worth it, even though being married to a farmer meant Jane ended up working two jobs most of her married life: one as a nurse and one as a helpmate on her husband's dairy farm. (Gordon, too, had an off-farm job, driving a school bus.)

"Gordon always said I married him for the farm, but I worked right along with him until he got sick in the nineties," she says. "Then we sold the cows and milk quota and bought beef cattle. I just hated that. It didn't matter that they had names and I made pets out of them; the consumer didn't care about that at all. But Gordon had heart trouble and mobility issues because of his arthritis so we needed to get animals I could handle."

Jane had always peppered the farm with other animals like sheep and goats she kept as pets, so they sold the beef cattle and expanded Jane's flock and herd. Gordon sold the lambs for meat but Jane focused her efforts on the wool. "We sold meat," Jane admits, "but my part of it was the fibre industry; we bred the sheep for wool and had angora goats for mohair, and cashmere goats for cashmere."

When even that became too much, Jane simply kept pleasure animals, which explains the horses, llamas, and sheep roaming the yard. (The couple also raised two sons, both of whom live in Ontario.) At the same time, Jane began thinking about her retirement. She knew one thing for sure: having worked as a full-time nurse since 1978, she wasn't going to sit around twiddling her thumbs.

"About five years before I knew I was going to retire—which I did in November 2012—I started to plan for those things I'd always wanted to do. Driving horses, keeping bees, and running a boarding kennel."

Fortunately, the infrastructure needed for the last part of Jane's retirement plan already existed; it just needed some renovations.

While his wife was working, Gordon had the dairy barn, with its concrete floors and insulated walls, converted into kennels. The former milk room became a grooming salon. That allowed Jane to indulge in another personal passion: rescuing animals.

"We always took in dogs that nobody wanted, that were abused or people threw away," Jane explains. "We love animals and we like being with them. I could make a pet out of anything," she says with a laugh.

In the end, Jane's retirement plan wasn't so much a change of profession as it was a change of clientele. It wasn't a big leap from health care to Litters 'n' Critters, a Nova Scotia-based organization that relies on foster families to take care of the dogs they rescue. Because of the conditions a lot dogs are found in, many go to Jane first. Her skills with grooming and nursing—as well as her ability to socialize dogs—are invaluable. Jane becomes both a dog's last resort and its first line of defense.

Jane's first mission with Litters 'n' Critters came with a public call for foster homes for puppies from the SPCA in Happy Valley-Goose Bay, Labrador, where resources for animals were very limited. When the shelter reached a crisis point in 2012, Jane was one of several volunteers who fostered the so-called "mushkadoodles." They arrived in Nova Scotia in a massive FedEx Canada airlift (a second airlift took place in 2013).

"Because I have the kennels, three bitches came here," Jane says. "One came with six pups, one whelped [gave birth] the day after she arrived, and one whelped a month later."

What she remembers most about the mothers was how they weren't used to having regular food. "They were eating twenty-one cups of kibble a day between the three of them," says Jane, who called the manager of the grocery store in nearby Pugwash to ask if there were any broken bags of kibble she could have at a discounted price.

"The next thing I knew, they brought us almost two thousand pounds of dog food. The building supplies [company] delivered it with their boom truck. It was amazing."

Those moments mean so much to a volunteer like Jane who sees what can happen to dogs at the hands of humans. She talks about Faith, a boxer-cross who was found tied to a tree in the woods and left to starve to death because she was pregnant, her skin a mess from dermatitis. She mentions another emaciated female trying to nurse her puppies while shut up in a small shed; her owner had gone to jail and his sister didn't want to spend money feeding his dog.

Seeing the abuse and neglect dogs endure is really hard on Jane, but the dogs' enduring spirits are part of what motivates her.

"I've never seen dogs so forgiving and so loving. We had a dog here a couple of years ago who was beautiful. He was big and blond and blue-eyed. He was gorgeous. He had been wrapped in barbed wire and stabbed sixteen times with a barbecue fork, then thrown away. Can you imagine?" she says with a scowl that would put the fear of Jane into any would-be animal abuser. "Somehow he crawled to where he could be rescued, and he came here. The only thing I found that made him nervous was the sound of steel dish hitting the cement; he would cringe. Otherwise, he was the most loving dog. He was adopted by a family with children and he's the star of their show."

Jane leans back in the salon's only chair, a swivel chair covered in dog hair Gordon needed to sit in when he helped her groom, and crosses her arms.

"We need to take a lesson from these dogs."

Sadly, Gordon passed away suddenly in 2014, two years after Jane retired. Now in her sixties, Jane admits she struggles without her partner and best friend. She misses his company but also his help with all the animals they both enjoyed caring for. Without Gordon, Jane simply can't add any more pets to a household already filled with eight dogs and numerous cats.

Surprisingly, only two of her dogs are kept rescues, including Bambi, who showed up at my home one evening, gaunt and covered in ticks. She had a porcupine quill stuck in her upper lip, preventing her from eating. We took her to the local vet who sent her to Jane's to recuperate; Bambi ended up being the last rescue dog Jane took in. I'm pleased Jane and I have something in common because truthfully, her unflagging work ethic and devotion to animals puts her in a league of her own; it's what keeps her going now that she is going it alone.

While it is far more difficult to do the dog grooming and boarding kennel and rescue volunteering on her own, Jane can't imagine giving any of it up, even though it's practically 24/7. More than one hundred rescue dogs have passed through her capable hands since 2012 and Jane isn't about to let the next hundred down.

"We have a responsibility to the animals," she says. "There are lots of people in this world who think of animals as a commodity, or product, or thing, and that's a mindset I cannot understand. It's really hard sometimes." She sighs and gives herself a little shake. "C'mon. Let's go meet the puppies."

We pass through the door separating the grooming salon from the kennel, and a cacophony of barking bounces off the concrete walls. Jane speaks quietly to each dog as she passes their kennels, but they keep barking at the stranger following her, whose face and smell they don't recognize. Jane opens up one kennel and a gaggle of four-week-old beagle puppies tumbles out, shooed by Jane to the door leading directly outside. As the pups run around the fenced-in area attached to the kennel building, Jane explains they came from a home where their mother was kept in a shed and their father was tied up.

"She looks like she's been nursing her whole life," Jane says, pointing to the mom, Sasha, who was strolling through the thick, green grass inside the enclosure. "She was being bred multiple times so her puppies could be sold. And the animal control officers thought the male was aggressive. I was going to turn him down but they already had him on the truck."

For Jane's safety, Duke, the father, arrived wearing a collar with a leash attached. When she took him into the fenced enclosure to see what he would do, he showed no signs of aggression whatsoever.

"He was chained so that might have been why he seemed aggressive to them. A chain changes their temperament," explains Jane. "Really, the whole family is adorable."

Although all the puppies and Duke are available for immediate adoption, Sasha, the mother, has to stay with Jane while she recuperates—first from nursing, then from being spayed.

"She would like it awful well if she could be with me all the time," Jane admits as she watches the mama dog sniff the grass. "She's so sweet."

That sweetness of temperament is often in stark contrast to the conditions in which the dogs are found. When she accepts rescued dogs to be groomed, kennelled, and taken care of, Jane is confronted with the worst of human nature. The situation from which the beagles came was one of the better stories. She recently helped with dogs from a puppy mill, whose fur was so matted with dirt and feces she had to cut most of the fur clean off.

"I cannot understand people who don't look at animals as living, important beings," Jane says. "I cannot understand why people don't get that dogs have the same thoughts and feelings we have and it's wrong not to take care of them."

As I squat down to take photos of the puppies, their calico fur contrasting sharply with the grass, they race over. One puppy takes my camera strap into his mouth and starts to pull.

"I love my job!" I say to Jane with a laugh, and she replies, "Gordon used to say this was a good way to satisfy my craving for fur." She smiles. "I get the chance to have all these dogs and puppies and not have to keep them. I don't have a hard time placing them but sometimes I have a hard time letting them go."

5

The Truth About Roadkill

e——— · • · ———ə

Most mornings between May and October, as long as it is light enough by seven o'clock, I head out along Route 301 for an hour's walk to Carrington Road and back. Route 301 is a well-travelled road and is busy in clusters around the top and bottom of the hour. During the first few months of my new life in the country, this road taught me an unforgettable lesson in life and death.

One damp morning in late June, as we approached the small white Presbyterian church by the creek, I noticed a raccoon lying on the faded white line marking the edge of the road. There was no blood or guts splashed over the asphalt, for which I was grateful; roadkill is sad enough without having to walk by its life spilled out on the road. I pulled the dog's leash tight to my side as we reached the carcass—this was Stella, after all, who loved to roll in dead stuff—but as we passed, the raccoon lifted its head.

The roadkill was not dead.

The raccoon swivelled its head towards us, its eyes grey and cloudy like the sky above us. They were the eyes of a suffering, dying creature. I scurried past, thinking it might attack us out of fear or pain, but it lay its head back down on the edge of the pavement. It didn't have the strength to crawl off the road into the grassy ditch, and I didn't have the fortitude or courage—or the gloves—to move it myself. I started to cry. It is hard enough to see a lifeless animal on the road, but it is truly upsetting to find out it is still alive and be unable to end its misery.

Most of us are familiar with roadkill; the dead animal streaked across the road or lying sideways on the shoulder. This road I walk each morning from spring to autumn is busy but sparsely populated and it runs through fields and woods—woods that are home to black bears, deer, coyotes, foxes, skunks, raccoons, and porcupines. Those who were here first. Those who are searching for new habitat as we cut down more and more forest.

On this morning, I felt profoundly ashamed to be one of the humans. Suddenly, I wondered how much of the roadkill we whiz past while averting our eyes is actually alive and suffering. As the dog and I returned home on the other side of the road, I promised myself I wouldn't look again. But as we came over the crest of the hill, my eyes sought the small black blob and couldn't leave it. On my side of the road, the spring calves were playing and I forced myself to keep watching them but as I came abreast of the raccoon, I couldn't help myself. I glanced over, hoping it was now dead.

"I'm sorry," I whispered. "Sorry, sorry, sorry."

Its body began twitching: the convulsions of the dying. In the forty minutes it took Stella and me to walk to Carrington Road and back, a dozen cars had passed. A dozen monstrous machines sped past this small raccoon where it lay at the edge of the asphalt. It lay there, feeling the vibrations build, having to endure every second of a car's approach and fly-by, not knowing if it was going to be struck again. Perhaps it would have been better if a vehicle put it out of its misery.

A few weeks later, during another morning walk, I spied a gaggle of ducklings milling about on the side of the road above the culvert.

It wasn't until the dog and I reached them that they got their act together and slipped down through the ditch to the safety of the creek. Until that moment, I was envisioning the look on my husband's face when he came home from work to find the bathtub full of baby ducks.

It's hard not to get attached to the wild animals in the neighbourhood, like the ospreys nesting on our property or the fox who raises her litter of pups on our riverbank lot across the road. Their comings and goings, their habits, and their hunting become familiar routines. I have enjoyed many a mug of coffee while watching the fox hunting in the field behind our house, admiring its black legs and red fur in sharp contrast against the white snow.

One morning about a year after the traumatizing raccoon incident, I sat on the top step of the back deck to tie my shoelaces before heading out for a walk and glanced up at the sun rising over the river. My eye caught a flash of movement in the green pasture next door: it was a fox, one of several living in our neighbourhood. It was young and healthy with a long, lean body and a distinct fluffy tail bobbing behind it. I watched as the fox arched its back, leaped straight up, pausing almost in mid-air, then landed with pinpoint accuracy. Breakfast caught.

Even though a fox made off with our first rooster within twenty-four hours of his arrival at our brand-new chicken coop, I don't despise the animals. Foxes are beautiful, intelligent creatures with whom I coexist. I do understand the cardinal rule of farm life: my first obligation is keeping my livestock safe and upholding that obligation may mean killing whatever creature threatens them. I am learning to accept that life and death go hand-in-hand in rural Nova Scotia: you watch a chick hatch and then you shoot a fox dead in the field.

The fox was long gone with its breakfast by the time the dog and I headed down the road for our walk. Halfway along, there is an abandoned house in one of the cow pastures and this summer, I'd watched a family of foxes cavorting over the old machinery and lumber left to rot along the edge of the orchard. As we approached this particular morning, a fox dashed across the road in front of us. He ran into the cow pasture and sat down. I stopped and we gazed across the fence at each other.

"Be careful on this road," I warned it. "Otherwise, you'll end up dead."

I held his stare, hoping to make him understand. Just stay off the road and you'll live, I thought. Just stay away from our property and you'll live.

Stella and I went on our way and the fox continued to watch us, his burnished triangle ears sticking out above the weeds.

A week later, at the same spot by the abandoned house, a fox lay on the road. It lay on its side, back feet entwined, ears limp. Its posture was one of rest after a night of hunting. A pool of red blood stained the asphalt under its mouth: a recent death.

"I'm sorry," I said out loud as we passed by.

Doomed to die either by gun or by car but always, it seemed, by human hands. I kept my eyes forward, remembering the agony of the raccoon. Stella sniffed the air but she did not pause, did not pull on the leash. A silver SUV, new and expensive, whizzed past me, confident in its ownership of the road. It sped by me so fast and so close it sucked the air out of me.

As we reached Carrington Road, Stella paused to sniff the body of a bird lying on the gravel shoulder.

"It's a cedar waxwing," I told her. "Poor bird."

We turned around and began heading back up the road. I glanced up at the overhead wires and recognized the silhouette perched there. A cedar waxwing.

"Your partner is back there," I said. "I'm sorry, I'm so sorry."

As we walked home, many cars passed us, people speeding to and from work. The closer we came to the abandoned house by the creek, the more I agonized over the condition of the fox body. We crested the hill and I could see the mound of red on the road ahead. A car passed up and then I saw its brake lights. I watched it swerve into the other lane. The car behind it did the same and so did the third car. Brake, swerve, avoid. This instinctive reaction is what made me cry.

I did not look at the fox as we walked by, my eyes blurred with tears. Instead I looked into the empty pasture where, just one week earlier, the fox had sat for our conversation, pointed red ears listening above the green, green grass.

6

Three O'clock
in the Morning

Cats are, generally, lovely creatures. They are undeniably cute when chasing leaves or moths, running up trees, and pawing at the door covered in snow. They are particularly cute when they curl up between your blanketed legs just as you are falling asleep in bed or when they climb onto your lap when you're reading a book to rub their chin against the spine. They are considerably less cute when they show up with a dead hummingbird proudly clamped between their jaws. No wonder I wake up in the middle of the night worrying about the hummingbirds (and all the other birds) living on our seemingly welcoming property.

Like any normal, twenty-first century person, I used to wake up at three o'clock every morning worrying about money, family, work, and the messy hall closet. Those things I understood; things we all worry about in our sleep. But when I started waking up in the middle of the night worrying about what the cat was up to—there had to be more to it. Surely there were more important things to fret over?

I Googled "Why do I wake up at 3:00 A.M.?" to see if there might be a physiological reason. Several sources suggested my middle of the night wake-up call came from my liver and was a sign of stress. Stress triggers the adrenal glands to give off adrenaline, which gives us a burst of energy to deal with whatever stressful situation we might be facing. Now apparently, the liver regenerates in the middle of the night and in order to do so, it requires glycogen (clusters of glucose that serve as energy storage in your body). The problem is adrenaline also uses glycogen, so if there are a lot of stressful situations in your life, your glycogen stores may be depleted when your liver is trying to regenerate overnight. If that's the case, the adrenal glands offer up adrenaline instead and—*bing!*—your eyes snap open and your brain immediately begins cataloguing worries. With everything going on in our lives and in the world, why would any sane person waste a perfectly good three o'clock wake-up call on a cat?

Because this particular cat has peed on you.

Like barns and the animals inside them, cats were not part of my upbringing. It's not that anyone in my family hated cats; we just didn't have them. Once my father retired, however, he decided he wanted cats and adopted two tabbies, a bonded pair, from the local shelter. They were indoor cats and perfectly content to lie on the windowsills of my parents' summer home, watching the cows in the field or the bees in the wild rose bushes. When I moved to rural Nova Scotia, I had little experience with outdoor cats of any kind: barn cats, stray cats, tree cats, ditch cats. Despite living in the country, my new husband didn't have any cats and didn't see the need for one. That is, until a young black-and-white cat started passing through our property; I named her Fern because I first spied her in a swath of ferns at the side of the house. She didn't come around often, likely because of Stella's enthusiastic greetings.

In early December, as the cold settled in, my husband said to me one morning over coffee, "I dreamt that black-and-white cat was in our house." The next day, I heard her meowing in the trees at the edge of our property. It took two feedings to get her to let me pat her and two more to accept our invitation inside.

No one said cats were stupid.

For the first year, Fern seemed perfectly content as a house cat. She decided a warm house and an easy food supply were preferable to life on the mean streets of our 'hood and she never indicated she wanted to go back outside. Since we have multiple bird feeders in our front yard, we didn't bother to suggest otherwise.

Everything went well until the following November. The combination of major house renovations and the arrival of a rambunctious puppy made Fern long for the great outdoors. When I didn't understand the messages she was sending to be let outside, she peed on our bed several mornings in a row. When I couldn't figure out why she was peeing on the bed, she peed on me. At three o'clock in the morning.

There I was, sitting in bed covered in pungent, quickly cooling cat piss wondering how to get the sheets off the bed without waking my husband.

"She's telling you she's not happy," explained my friend Jane, a lifelong cat person with six felines of her own. "She wants to be outside."

Thus began my new job of opening and closing a door fifty times a day just to keep the cat happy and avoid her peeing on me again. Once Fern was able to go outside, everything was stress-free.

Unless you were a bird.

Cats, apparently, are the leading cause of death for birds. More than windows and buildings, more than power lines, more than cars, trucks, and airplanes. It's mostly feral cats doing the killing but our sweet, cuddly, well-fed pets are keeping pace; it's estimated cats kill almost 200 million birds each year. And that's just in Canada: the numbers in the United States could be in the billions.

And you wonder why I woke up at three o'clock in the morning worrying about this?

My sweet little tuxedo cat with her green eyes, white whiskers, and teeny-tiny voice, was a relentless predator and I carried all the guilt that went along with that because my husband and I are serious bird lovers. We started feeding the birds our first winter together (about four years before Fern arrived) and within weeks, Dwayne called buying birdseed his new addiction.

"I might have to give up smoking to afford this," he quipped as he unloaded two more fifteen-kilogram bags of striped sunflower seed from his truck. (It has occurred to me, in a brief moment of weakness, that if cats weren't killing all those birds, we might have gone bankrupt buying birdseed.)

That first winter, we kept a list of the birds hanging around our feeders—we had sixteen different species, including pine grosbeaks and red crossbills. But once Fern started roaming around outside again, the variety disappeared; we never saw those grosbeaks or crossbills again.

It was hard enough to cope with birds slamming into our large picture window without knowing that Fern was sitting below waiting to scoop up the stunned finch or sparrow. I once spent an hour apologizing to a male grosbeak I'd rescued from inside the garage after I realized it was his female counterpart I'd found on the back lawn and buried earlier that day.

It wasn't a lack of glycogen waking me up at three o'clock in the morning now, but a full dose of guilt. And maybe the tiny feathered ghosts of birds killed by Fern. At this point, I thought about getting up to clean and organize the hall closet.

As the puppy grew up and lost interest in the cat, Fern seemed to settle down and stay inside more. It was a relief to know she was stalking and killing fewer birds but my relief was short-lived. Now, instead of fretting about the global carnage of birds, I could start worrying about my pets contracting Lyme disease.

When you move to the country and learn about ticks dropping off branches and viruses infesting puddles, you really have to wonder if it isn't safer living in the city. By the time I found the tick on Fern's throat, it was the size of a dime. It was summertime, so she wasn't spending much time indoors and only allowed us to pat her occasionally; this tick had ample time to feast. Since ticks were a whole new kettle of bug for this city girl, I picked up the phone knowing I could count on the person on the other end, even at seven-thirty in the morning.

"Fern has tick on her. How do I take it off?"

"I'll be right there," Jane replied.

While I held Fern, Jane took the large tick between the nails of her thumb and forefinger and, with a quick *snick*, popped it off the cat.

"That's disgusting! You used your fingers," I shrieked by way of thanks.

She put the tick, its black legs wiggling at the top of its engorged grey body, on the counter and I put a dime next to it. Same size.

"Now *that's* disgusting," Jane said.

Months later, when what I thought was a skin tag on Stella turned out to be an engorged tick, I made another phone call, this one at nine o'clock at night.

"Stella has a tick on her. Will you take it off?"

(Just so you know, this behaviour is totally in character for me. The year we went to Disney World with my sister and her family, one of my nephews came up to me holding out his arm. There was a small red tick trying to burrow into his skin. "Go see your mother," I told him.)

Now, I fully understand the concept of learning to do something yourself, I really do, but since my husband's suggestion was to burn the tick off with a cigarette, I had to turn to Jane for help. As competent as she was, Jane just used her thumbnail. I have two issues employing this technique myself. One: ew. And two: with my luck I'd break the head off, which defeats the whole purpose of removing a tick. If the head is left in the skin, so too are the salivary glands and that's where the bacteria that causes Lyme disease are secreted.

Here's the thing about country living and being a competent country girl, however: when there's a lesson you have to learn, the rural universe just keeps lobbing the opportunities your way.

When a tick inevitably showed up on my younger dog—she spends a lot of time running through the woods—it was engorged enough to be visible, but not big enough to gross me out completely. Besides, like finding a dead chicken in the coop, after two or three, you become desensitized to the creepiness. Also like finding a dead chicken in the coop, I realized it was time for me to learn to how to deal with ticks myself. If my cat and dogs were going to be outside, it was clear ticks would be an ongoing problem. I needed a solution before Jane started answering her phone with, "Jane's Expert Tick Removal: you tick 'em, I snick 'em," and sending me invoices.

Turns out, the vet had a nifty little gadget to remove a tick—head and all—with a few gentle turns, no thumbnail or tweezers required. Slick enough to quell any squeamishness and prevent any more three o'clock wake-up calls. It wasn't long before an opportunity to try out my handy-dandy "tick twister-outer" presented itself.

A week later, I found a small tick on the back of Fern's neck. Instead of picking up the phone, I picked up the gadget, clamped the pincher on the tick, and gently turned two or three times. The tick, with its wiggling legs and ugly little head, slid out of my cat's skin. Victory!

When I lived in the city, the only thing I worried about biting my dog was the terrier at the dog park. Now I'm pulling ticks off my pets like I'm employee of the month at Jane's Expert Tick Removal. That certainly helps me sleep at night. And I've crossed another item off the "How to be a Country Girl" list.

7

Funeral for a Mouse

⸻ · •• ⸻

There are very few lines from Mary Oliver's poetry that don't make me gasp. An American poet in her eighties, who is, as I write this sentence, living and publishing, Mary Oliver astounds poetry lovers—and makes people love poetry—because she writes simply and profoundly about the natural world.

When a family friend died suddenly and tragically in late April a few years ago, it was Oliver's poem "Wild Geese" that answered my call to understand: "Tell me about despair, yours, and I will tell you mine./Meanwhile the world goes on."

Likely, no matter what situation you are facing—what loss you are enduring, what hope you are clinging to—Mary Oliver has a poem, or a line, for you. I wonder what she would have been inspired to write had she been around when my niece and nephews, visiting Nova Scotia from Atlanta, came rushing up the stairs to the front deck buzzing with excitement.

The eldest boy, George, who was eight at the time, had something in his hand. His brothers and sister wanted to see it again, and they wanted to show me. When George unfurled his fingers, a hummingbird lay in his palm.

"It died, Aunt Sa," George said in his serious voice. "Can we bury it?"

We had to; otherwise, the kids' jostling to hold the bird was going to see it torn into pieces. Or one of the kids would drop the bird and our ten-month-old pup would snatch it up and take off. Both were indignities I hoped to spare this poor hummingbird.

"Yes, we can bury it. Let's put it under the phlox," I answered George and fetched a small shovel from the garden shed. I also scooped up some rose petals.

I dug a small hole and George placed the hummingbird on the moist soil. Natan and Vinny placed the rose petals over the body and I covered it all with dirt. My niece, Mimi, appeared with a small stone to mark the grave. We sat together on the grass in silence for a short while and then George asked, "Is it bones yet?"

If you want to have a candid and thought-provoking conversation, sit down with an eight-year-old. The conversations are deep, but short. You need to pay attention, be honest, and try not to overthink. Children ask tough questions, but that doesn't intimidate me (at least not until the fifth "why?" in a row). But because I don't have children of my own, I don't have those built-in parental controls so I sometimes worry about providing more detail than a child can handle or more information than her parents might be comfortable with. In this case, though, I know my sister, Araminta, is open and honest with her children so there's little I can say that will upset them or her.

Besides, if we're going to shield our children from bad things, dying and death shouldn't be one of them—especially if you're hanging out in the country, where anything and everything can wind up dead on your doorstep. Death is natural and unavoidable for people, pets, and wild animals. When a fox snatched our pet chicken the year before, these kids sent a homemade condolence card. Fifteen years of observation and interaction with my friends' kids taught me children are smarter, more thoughtful, and more resilient when it comes to accepting reality than many adults.

Children are inquisitive, fearless, and capable of experiencing a full range of emotion without being permanently traumatized. Sadness is a part of life and a healthy, compassionate emotion to express at any age. Granted, some children develop their emotional depth very early. George, for instance, was born with a congenital heart defect and underwent open-heart surgery when he was three months old. He lives with the knowledge that the arteries going in and out of his heart won't grow like they are supposed to. My youngest nephew, Vinny, was only a year old when his only living grandfather, my dad, passed away; he is growing up hearing stories and seeing photos of the "Papa" he'll never meet. George, Mimi, Natan, and Vinny have an adopted sister who is globally and developmentally delayed; Lovey does not see or hear or speak and will never grow larger than a toddler. She lives in a slowly progressing state of palliative care, and her siblings understand her health issues and know she will die some day.

When my sister receives news that someone special to her has died—like our family friend a few Aprils ago—she doesn't hide her tears from her children; she simply explains why she is crying. Instead of sheltering her children from the reality of illness and death, Araminta is helping them identify and live with those realities in their lives without anxiety or grief. Instead, they learn to appreciate every moment, every joy, every day. That openness makes them fearless yet considerate about the corpses they discover on our rural property.

Later that same afternoon, the kids found a mouse the cat had killed. Being the grandchildren of Papa, who was a funeral director, this time they wanted a more formal send-off. First off, they wanted this grave under one of the maple trees.

As Vinny, who was four, waited as I dug the hole, he held the red plastic shovel carrying the body.

"I'm so-wee," he murmured, bent close over the mouse. "I wuv you."

When he leaned in to kiss the mouse, however, I intervened. Even Aunt Sa knows the limitations to a child's expression of feelings.

Ever been to a funeral for a mouse?

We placed the mouse in the freshly dug hole under the maple tree, in between two thick roots. We had a eulogy, which was simply everyone talking all at once about their favourite memory of the mouse, so it lasted about two minutes. Mimi had expanded her grave-marker business into decorated headstones; she offered up another flat rock on which she had written "RIP" in black Sharpie, and drawn a portrait of the mouse underneath.

But most importantly, there were bubbles. I don't know where they came from, whether the kids brought them or slipped away for them, but suddenly they produced their bottles and wands and proceeded to blow bubbles above the mouse's grave. It was the nicest funeral I've been to: it wasn't the least bit upsetting. The afternoon sun shone through the maple branches and the bubbles sparkled as they floated in the air around us, making it feel like a celebration of life.

We ended up burying two more bodies that day, with less ritual. I'm glad I'd warned the kids that sometimes the cat eats the head of a mouse it kills because when they found a headless rodent, they took it in stride. We now had several rocks scattered throughout the flower gardens with "RIP" and a mouse face drawn on them.

"No more interments until next summer, okay?" I finally declared and went inside to pour myself a restorative glass of red wine.

A couple of days later, a friend came over. "Why are there stones with 'RIP' and a mouse face drawn on them sitting by your garage door?" she wanted to know.

I didn't really have an answer for that question. Apparently, the kids had made up extra headstones, understanding that one should be prepared for death. Just in case, I suppose. Just in case.

I wonder if Mary Oliver has ever been to a funeral for a mouse. If she hasn't, she would have loved the one these kids created that July afternoon in our front yard.

She might write a poem about it but for now, these lines from her poem "sometimes" will suffice:

Instructions for living a life:
Pay attention.
Be astonished.
Tell about it.

So here's my poem, "burying birds," with thanks (or apologies) to Mary Oliver:

Instructions for conversing with kids:
Pay attention.
Be honest.
Don't overthink.

Meanwhile, when I am done living this life—having paid attention, been astonished, and told you all about it—I don't want a lot of tears at my funeral. Kiss me, tell me you wuv me, share your favourite memory, then bury me in the field behind the house and blow bubbles while wild geese fly overhead, looking for a place to land on the river.

8

Deer to My Heart

⸺ ⸱⸱⸱ ⸺

When my niece was four years old, she learned how to write her name. All of a sudden, she was able to sign "Mimi" on every picture she drew. Her mother then taught her how to draw hearts, so Mimi went through a phase of adding one under every signature.

Around the same time, I read in an article in a women's magazine about how a deer's hoofprints often resemble hearts as drawn by young children. Having never seen either, I had no reference point. Yet now that I lived in the country and watched deer walking across the field behind our house daily, this idea appealed to me.

Shortly after, an envelope arrived from Georgia, where my sister lives, filled with drawings by my niece and nephew. On the back of her drawing, Mimi had signed her name and drawn a heart: a perfect, hoof-shaped heart.

Talk about serendipity.

At the time, I simply made the connection and kept Mimi's drawing, although—foolishly—not the article. When it came time to write about this a few years later, I searched every notebook, every folder, and every pile of papers in my office, but I could not locate the idea or its author. I was sure it belonged to American nature writer Rick Bass so I emailed him; he replied that while a lovely idea, it was not one of his.

While I won't take credit for the idea, I have claimed it because I've proven it. Perhaps the way it happened—reading the quote then receiving Mimi's drawing—made the connection indelible to me because after that, I began to look at the deer tracks in the mud or snow differently. Everywhere I looked, I began to see hoofprints that looked like my niece's hand-drawn heart.

Tracks are easy to find in winter, the snow a blank canvas for deer, fox, rabbits, mice, crows, pheasants, and occasionally the wing-tips of partridge. Sometimes I worry as I walk around our property with my head down, eyes searching the ground, that I'm not paying attention to everything around me. The truth is, though, my senses are engaged.

My ears are tuned to the call of the pileated woodpecker, the sound of water running under the snow, or the *whump-whump* of raven wings cutting through the cold morning air. My nose draws in the sweet smell of the barely frozen soil while my hands tingle from the chill. The sharp needles of the Norway spruce trees prick my fingers as I push the branches aside. Every step makes me feel acutely alive and grateful to be living in this wide-open space of grass and trees and clouds.

To begin seeing hearts on this property simply reinforced another, longer-held suspicion: this move to the east coast was the right one. I walked a lot when I lived in Vancouver—occasionally in the forests with huge west coast trees and once a week along the beach—but more often than not, my senses were tuned to the sounds of cars and buses and delivery trucks, to the smells of restaurants and exhaust, and to the feel of my feet pounding asphalt and concrete.

A week before moving to Nova Scotia in March 2007, I stepped out of a coffee shop with a large cappuccino in my hand; I'd not bothered to put a lid on my foamy drink. I took a sip then looked down. The tilting action of my sip had caused the cinnamon and foamed milk to swirl into the shape of a heart. I stood in the parking lot and searched for someone, anyone, to share the discovery with. For once, there was no one nearby; likely I saved myself the embarrassment of accosting a perfect stranger and explaining why I was excited about seeing the shape of a heart in my cappuccino foam. That heart was totally random but it seemed like a good omen; it seemed like a simple affirmation of my decision to follow my heart to a life in rural Nova Scotia...and to Dwayne.

The first time I came across a line of heart-shaped hoofprints in the snow, it reminded me of my niece and how much I missed her, how I wished I could share these walks with her. She's bright and creative and athletic and she picks up new ideas very quickly. I wanted to show her the connection she created for me with deer.

That connection would take on more significance when I found out, two weeks before Christmas 2013, that the sixty-five acres of woods next to our property were going to be cut down that winter. It was devastating: those woods were only separated from our property by an old, unmaintained road, and were a big part of my enjoyment of my walks along that road. The clear-cutting, which levelled nearly all the trees, lasted three long months.

While it was upsetting to my husband and me—he who had lived alongside those woods his entire adult life—it wasn't just humans who were affected. Many birds and animals found shelter, sustenance, and homes amongst those sixty-five acres of poplar and pine trees. The piles of logs next to the road did a good job of hiding the flattened woods but once they were hauled away, my heart ached every time I looked across the wasteland that had once been a thick, living community of trees.

Despite the destruction of habitat and view, the clear-cut did achieve something good that winter of 2014, when the snow was deep and several ice storms had glazed the trees and snow with a thick crust. The birds and mammals were having a tough time. As a result of the clear-cut, all the treetops ripped from trunks and left lying on the ground provided easily accessible food for deer.

Humans love to complain about the weather and how tough winter is but white-tailed deer have it immeasurably harder. Deep snow makes it difficult for them to move around and find food, and the younger they are, the more of a struggle it is. Deer are herbivores. They have four stomachs to help them squeeze out as much nutrition from their diet of grass and leaves as possible, so life is challenging enough during an average winter.

The abundance of fresh, easily accessible treetops meant there were a lot of deer roaming the field behind our home. Dozens of deer, the most we'd ever seen. They are beautiful, graceful, and skittish animals, and their very presence was a balm to my heart as I watched them from the house. But it wasn't just their rounded ears, dark eyes, flashy white tails, and leaping legs that soothed my hurting heart, it was what they left behind: hundreds of hoofprints. Hundreds of hearts.

Every day, our hearts beat about 100,000 times, sending over 7,500 litres of blood coursing through our bodies. Every day, our hearts create enough energy to power a truck for 32 kilometres. (That's about the distance between the town of Oxford and the town of Amherst, or the approximate distance from Mount Saint Vincent University to Halifax Stanfield International Airport.) The heart is the source and maintenance of life, and a good heart means good health—it's little wonder we associate hearts with love.

Long before my unknown author of the magazine article realized child-drawn hearts resemble deer hoofprints, we had created a heart symbol to represent the feelings associated with it. The heart symbol we use today has its roots in the eleventh and twelfth centuries, when European art—both secular and religious—began depicting a person handing over their heart to a lover or to Jesus Christ.

The first representation of a stylized heart in art was a pine cone, point up, which was apparently in accordance with medieval anatomical descriptions of the organ. Around the fourteenth century, this image was flipped, point down, and over time it became the standard graphic we see everywhere today to represent love. Including on the old road beside our property.

So, it was absolutely worth following my heart to the country to marry a man who replanted every acre of trees he cut down around his house. I remember standing in his kitchen on our third or fourth date, looking at the Manitoba maple spreading its limbs and leaves all over the front yard, and thinking, "I feel perfectly at home in this house, among all these trees."

Deer follow their hearts as well, through the woods in the mud of spring or the snow of winter, along paths that lead them to food and safety. Following their hoofprints—a trail of hearts—home.

Every time I come across deer tracks on the old road alongside our house into the remaining woods, I search until I find one that looks like my niece's drawing. Taking off my glove, I lay my palm flat on top of it, the heat of my skin melting the snow, until my hand rests against the cold, hard ground. The heart disappears, absorbed, becoming as much a part of my senses as the wings in the air, the water under the earth, and the air in my lungs.

9

The Face of Timeless Devotion

⸎ —— · ·· —— ⸎

*I*t's an unmistakable face, the face of an old dog. The white muzzle, the white hairs in the eyebrows, a pair of rheumy eyes beneath that may or may not be clear yet still sparkle, tuffs of white inside ever-listening ears. The face of an old dog is one we love particularly well, the opposite of the cute puppy face. We cradle this face, look more closely at it, and try to remember when it was all black or all brown or just not quite so…white.

When we look at a human being with white hair and wrinkles, we don't immediately think with compassion, even empathy, that time is pawing closely at that person. Yet a dog whose face has whitened means only one thing: heartbreak and farewell are surely around the corner.

The face of an old dog suggests "short-evity" as opposed to long-evity; a brutal reminder that the creature we love so deeply—and who loves us back unconditionally—will soon surrender her job of greeting us at the door. This knowledge gives us our humanity and keeps us humble about our role in a dog's life. It makes us profoundly grateful for this strange mix of blessings on four legs. In our dogs, we see responsibility for a good life and death, for everlasting love, and enduring heartache. In our dogs, we see ourselves, our future, and the inevitable.

If we are lucky, we see this several times. We choose to go through this over and over again: holding an old dog in our arms, saying goodbye while dripping tears into that beloved fur, vowing to never do it again...and then eventually feeling longing tug on us like a leashed dog wanting to run free. Every dog is a journey of hope.

When my older dog, Stella, turned ten, the double digits made me aware of approaching the end of the road. It could have been miles away or just around the corner; there was no way of knowing.

The road we walked together was not easy. Stella arrived a year after my first dog, Maggie, died and was buried on Pugwash Point. As an eight-month-old puppy, Stella came into my life when I was going through a divorce and helping to take care of a father with dementia. Going through that emotional tumult together, especially in her first three years, put her protective instincts and dominant nature into overdrive. Our battles for dominance and control—in the fields of Pugwash Point and the streets of Cobourg, Ontario—were legendary, if only to me, the human at the other end of the leash who wanted a quiet, well-behaved dog instead of one who pulled me down the street like a greyhound chasing a rabbit.

We moved to Nova Scotia when Stella was four, where she joined a (much-needed) human alpha male on his huge rural property. The space helped mellow us both out, although we still revisited old battles periodically, the not-coming-when-called-because-this-rotting-carcass-needs-rolling-in skirmish being the most common. We also created new battles, like how much chicken poop she should be eating, or how she claimed the best armchair because it was in the sun with a view of the driveway (which is why it was my reading chair). They were more benign skirmishes now that the chaos of youth had given way to the routine of middle age.

Age did nothing to diminish Stella's obsession with food, however. When Stella was almost ten, we introduced a puppy, Abby, into the house. Aware of the politics of hierarchy and dominance among canines, I always fed Stella, the incumbent, first. Every morning as I prepared the younger dog's breakfast, I said to Stella, "Get out of the kitchen. You are not getting a second breakfast." It was a (one-sided) conversation we had every single morning, as if Stella hoped one day there would indeed be a second breakfast.

If ever a dog was food-oriented, it was Stella. A construction worker in Vancouver had introduced this terminology to me on afternoon as I walked by with my first boxer, Maggie. As we reached this construction worker sitting on the bumper of a truck eating a sandwich, Maggie plunked down in front of him and stared. He looked at the dog. Then he looked at me.

"Is your dog food-oriented?" he asked.

There she sat, a thick-chested, pumpkin-headed, sixty-five-pound boxer with a square jaw and a steady gaze. It was clear that we would go no further until he shared a bite of his sandwich.

After five years in Vancouver, Maggie and I returned home to the east coast and during the summer, a vet discovered cancer throughout her nine-year-old body. Every evening for the final week of her life, I loaded Maggie into the car and we drove along the shore with the windows down, the smell of the sea wafting through the backseat, then stopped at the ice cream stand on the way home so she could eat an orange-pineapple baby cone.

Every morning, I lifted her up onto my bed so she could take her pain medication and share my banana: a bite for her, a bite for me. On her final morning, the last tastes in her mouth were banana, a piece of toast covered in peanut butter, and my breath as I held her close while the vet injected her.

A few months after Maggie's death, my parents' ten-year-old dog started passing blood in her poop. When he couldn't find anything obviously wrong with her, the vet recommended a temporary diet of cooked ground beef and rice. I remembered what Maggie had taught me: dogs are food-oriented. I remembered what I'd read: feeding a dog kibble was like a human eating a hamburger and fries for every meal. The dog's new diet didn't end up being temporary. Why not give her the food every dog obviously craves—and is willing to steal?

Back in 2002, cooking "human food" for dogs was an are-you-kidding-you're-wasting-perfectly-good-food-on-a-dog commitment. For some reason, people felt feeding a dog ground beef, rice, green beans, yogurt, and an egg was "wasting food." Yet, on a steady diet of "human food," my parents' dog lived another three years.

Unfortunately, when Stella the puppy arrived, I was still stuck in my old ways and believed she had to be on kibble "specially formulated for a puppy" until she was one year old. Calling Stella "very active" is a polite way of saying she was wild and crazy. Stella needed better food to burn in her very busy body. Wiser now, I would have fed her steak and sweet potatoes until I couldn't count every rib (my mother took to calling her "Ribsy") but back then, I missed the signs that Stella was starving.

"Where did the blueberry muffins go?" my mother asked one afternoon during Stella's second year at our summer house in Nova Scotia.

She assumed I'd put them away for her. I looked at Stella. My mother looked at Stella. The low counter in the house's pantry kitchen made it too easy. Stella's poops had half-digested paper muffin cups in them for days.

This happened regularly until we finally got it through our heads to push baking or thawing meat as far back on the counter as possible, then barricade it behind oven mitts and timers and salt and pepper shakers for good measure.

It was after we'd moved my father into a nursing home that I met Dwayne and married him. Stella promptly endeared herself to my new husband by eating a pound of raw haddock off the tray before he had a chance to barbecue it.

"It was on the counter," he growled.

I shrugged. He'd learn.

Stella was a thief who wasn't sneaky or remorseful. She didn't skulk and she never had that guilty look other dogs get when they know they've done something wrong. Stella's expression seemed to say "whatever," and she said it as she licked her jowls.

The only thing that stopped her was spondylosis: the degeneration of her spine prevented her from putting her front legs up on the counter. Nevertheless, the habit of barricading food as far back from the edge as possible was ingrained.

In the autumn of both the year and her life, eleven-year-old Stella, the now three-year-old pup, and I walked down the road to visit my husband's parents. As I was chatting with my eighty-eight-year-old father-in-law in another room, I spied Stella—fat, old, lazy Stella, her spiny vertebrae visible under her fur—with her front paws on the low counter in my in-laws' century-old kitchen, her mouth around a package of donuts.

"Oh, that's okay," my father-in-law chuckled when I apologized. "She's like me, she knows those donuts are good."

He hobbled to the kitchen and grabbed the mangled package.

"Stella, we might as well eat all of these now," he said, sitting down at the table. Stella sat down next to him, thick-chested, pumpkin-headed, and food-oriented.

And why not? In human years, my dog was almost the same age as my father-in-law. If you can't eat whatever you want by the time you hit your eighties, what's the point in living that long?

Once Stella was firmly entrenched as an old dog, her needs governed our house. Stella got to eat first. Stella got to sprawl across the entire couch. Stella got to resist going outside in the cold or the rain but still got a biscuit because the door opened. Strong and willful as a young dog, Stella simply became an older, fatter, and lazier version of herself. *Whatever.* And after twelve years together, Stella was my seven o'clock and my five o'clock. She was the routine that defined my day and the dog that defined my mid-life.

In a collection of essays about dogs by E. B. White, author of the classic children's book *Charlotte's Web*, he says of his old dachshund, Fred: "Life without him would be heaven, but I am afraid this is not what I want." When I looked into Stella's familiar, frustrating face, I wasn't sure how I would feel when I held her in my arms and felt her life end. Stella was a larger-than-life kind of dog, both memorable and challenging, and she would leave a gaping hole in our home and my heart. I figured I would appreciate her more when she was gone, unfortunately, but I was also afraid that was not what I wanted.

In the last year of her life, my favourite Stella moments were those days she ran through the field, grinning her unique toothy grin. These are the moments that gladden the heart of any companion of an old dog: when she forgets whatever aches are bothering her to indulge the pleasures of playing, exploring, of accompanying, of being the dog she once was. These moments are bittersweet; the fact they do not occur daily reminds us how age is affecting her body, and recalls the dog who came before her…and how we went through all this back then.

But always together. To the very last breath from that soft, white muzzle—holding on to our dignity and hers as best we can—the dog is more accepting and gracious about her death than we will ever be.

Stella: March 2003–April 2015

10

Ma'am, Back Away from the Goats

Two grown women hanging out with the goats at the Magnetic Hill Zoo near Moncton, New Brunswick, seemed to make the other parents nervous. It's not as if there were no other grown-ups in the petting enclosure; it's just we were the only ones without children. And we were spending more time with the goats than the (human) kids were.

My friend Jane and I had talked about going to the zoo for ages so I finally decided we'd go during her week's vacation in September. We picked a sunny day and headed off to visit the lions and tigers. The petting goats were an unexpected surprise.

It's my fault we hung out with the goats so long; I was getting my goat fix. Six months earlier I had spent two days at my friend

Heather's dairy goat farm in Blockhouse, near Mahone Bay, and met her Swiss Toggenburgs. I fell in love.

"They are just like dogs," Heather had said as she introduced me to her herd of large, friendly goats. That was all I needed to hear.

Jane had already primed my interest by telling me that, when she was ten, her family had moved to a property in Oxford Junction along the River Philip, and her mother started a small herd of milking goats. Over the first three years of our friendship, Jane had filled me with details about helping her mother with the herd. Of course, my favourite story featured the newborn kids going inside the house for bottle-feeding.

If I ever do get a wee herd of these entertaining ungulates, my goat guru and milking mentor will be Jane: she who almost got us arrested at the petting-goat enclosure.

A couple of the pygmy goats looked very wide around the belly and I asked Jane if they were pregnant.

"Let me check," she said, then proceeded to squat down behind one of the goats and grab her udder.

This is what you need to know about Jane: she's fearless, outspoken, and competent. If someone wants to know if a goat is pregnant or if a newly adopted kitten is infested with fleas, Jane will investigate, then fix or solve. Frankly, it's one of the reasons our friendship works. I tend to attract competent people into my life.

As Jane checked out the goat's udder, a man with two young girls looked at Jane. Then he looked at the goat. Then he looked back at Jane.

"It's okay," I reassured him. "She knows what she's doing."

My words didn't register because he remained in flight-or-fight mode, as induced by watching a grown woman fondle a goat in the petting enclosure.

"She grew up with goats," I explained. "She's just trying to figure out if that goat is pregnant."

The man blinked. Then he laughed. "Oh, I see. Okay, then, I was wondering…."

"Her udder is firm," Jane announced right then, "so there's milk in there."

The man took a few steps closer to his daughters.

Oddly, what Jane was doing didn't embarrass me; I was fascinated by her hands-on efficiency and her knowledge of the workings of an udder. I completely forgot we were in a petting enclosure, not Jane's backyard. This ease with animals, this knowledge of their bodies, cycles, and abilities are things I long to possess.

If you're raised in the city and no one in your family has a farm, if you don't have a best friend who is horse-crazy and invites you to ride with her, if you've never heard of the 4-H organization, then you never get a chance to hang around large animals. Sure, you might see them at the Roseneath Fair, the provincial exhibition, or the Royal Agricultural Winter Fair, but you admire them from a distance and wrinkle your nose at the smell. For most people, not hanging around with large farm animals isn't a problem; milk and meat come from the grocery store, eggs rest in cartons, and chickens are headless, featherless, and boneless. But even as I wrinkled my nose as I walked in a barn or pulled my hand back from the groping lips of a horse, there was always an underlying craving for the opposite experience.

When I was nine, our minister in Ontario invited my family to visit him one summer in Pugwash, where he was born and raised. When we arrived, we met his brother who owned a dairy farm and had a daughter, Sue, the same age as me. This became not only our annual family vacation, but also my annual attempt at being a farm girl. What I admired most about my new friend was her confidence with the cows and horses. Yet no matter how many vacations I spent trailing after Sue, listening to her stories, and watching her work, I never learned to be as comfortable as she was around the big mouths, large hooves, and switching tails.

Ironically, if it hadn't been for my mother's extreme allergy to horses, I might have taken up riding as a teenager. Raised in the country and a lover of animals both wild and domesticated, my father would have supported either of his daughters' interest in riding. But we grew up knowing it was not an option.

My husband, Dwayne, was raised on a working farm, first with milking cows providing cream, then a small herd of beef cattle. He even had his own pet cow, a heifer he named Herman. Alas, by the time I came around, the cows were long gone and the barns too full of junk to be used. When his father gave him seventy-two acres just up the road from his childhood farm, my husband never got around to building his own barn. I think he's secretly relieved because now we don't have one for me to fill with animals.

Despite these facts, I would like to have farm animals around me, to feed and clean them. I would like to learn about the world through their eyes. I've even come to appreciate the pungent smell of fresh manure and no longer wrinkle my nose when I step into a barn. In fact, I've started to inhale deeply.

On the other hand, I admit I have no idea how to take care of farm animals, even hobby ones. Everything I read by authors who actually keep sheep, cows, and donkeys—how come no one writes about goats?—keeps my eyes open and my feet firmly planted in the barnyard when it comes to the demanding, sometimes harsh, realities of farming.

Shortly after I moved to Nova Scotia from Ontario, I read *The Good Good Pig: The Extraordinary Life of Christopher Hogwood* by Sy Montgomery, who lives in rural New Hampshire and wrote about the runt piglet she adopted after his original owner couldn't bear to put him down. As a result of that book, my lifelong dream of having a pet pig—fuelled by years of watching the movie *Babe*—died. I discovered the truth about pigs: if not butchered at six months, they can grow to five hundred pounds. Through Montgomery's story, I discovered how much food it takes to feed a creature that size, and how a pig uses its nose to carve plate-sized chunks out of lawns; I knew I couldn't handle the former and Dwayne wouldn't be pleased by the latter.

Fortunately, my husband was not to blame for squelching that dream. Instead, he made another one come true by building a chicken coop in the backyard so I could hear a rooster crowing every morning (one of the sounds I craved while living in Vancouver and listening to car alarms and sirens). Unfortunately for my husband, the coop didn't quite squelch my hankering for animals; chickens are lovely, but they are small and feathery and require little care. You watch a chicken more than you interact with it. You certainly don't gaze into a chicken's eyes to learn the secrets of the animal kingdom.

So when I started making noise about getting goats and a donkey, maybe a pair of sheep to keep the lawn mowed, and ooh! How about a llama, honey? My husband finally said, "When you make more money, you can have more animals." A savvy negotiation since I am a freelance writer, and not a very prolific one.

Livestock yearnings aside, I *am* smart enough to know that I'm not smart enough to keep goats. It's possible to learn about dogs, horses, goats, or goldfish through books and people like my friend Jane, but I simply don't have the time or the money to turn myself into a proper goat keeper. Besides, if there were ever a goat born with the hankering to hang out on the hood of a car, that's the goat I'd get.

But that didn't stop me from spending too much time in the goat enclosure at the zoo. I figured my education had to start somewhere and the number one item on this city girl's (revised) wish list was this: learn how to grope an udder to determine if there's milk inside. And do it without getting kicked. There is an art to udder fondling, I'm sure, and it has to do with the confidence that comes from growing up with animals; a confidence Jane, Dwayne, Sue, and Heather all have.

If I had to pinpoint one perspective-altering influence of my country life, it would be the in-your-face-ness of the birds and the bees. By which I mean the "birds" and the "bees." There is no farmer, no keeper—of any age—of horses, goats, cows, or rabbits who isn't familiar with animal genitalia, and more importantly, their purpose. You don't get milk or babies if your animals don't get pregnant. And if you want to ensure everything functions as it should, you have to inspect the equipment and watch the process. That means observing both ends of it: the procreation and the product. It doesn't get more basic and practical than that, and you can't be squeamish or nervous or giggly about it.

So I was quite proud of my friend Jane as she fondled the goat's udder at the Magnetic Hill Zoo's petting enclosure, trying to answer the question I'm sure other grown-ups visiting the goats with their children were asking themselves.

"I really want a pet goat," I said as we finally left the petting enclosure and headed over to the otters who were just as cute but, regrettably, untouchable.

"You have no idea," Jane shook her head.

The spring following our trip to the zoo, Heather, my friend with the dairy goats in Blockhouse, sent me a message. She also keeps a herd of Alpine goats for weed and brush control and a kid from that spring's litter had developed septicemia and was now blind. She knew about my interest in goats and wrote, "She would make a good pet."

Talk about tugging hard on the heartstrings of a wannabe farm girl.

"We need to have a serious conversation about this," I said to my husband. "I don't want you to dismiss it out of hand; I want to really consider this."

So I told him about the blind baby doeling, and asked him if there was any reason not to bring her home.

He looked at me and said, very sweetly and gently (and, I truly believe, with a bit of regret), "We don't have a proper barn for it to live in during the winter."

And you know, I understood that: I didn't want to make a commitment with the best of intentions but not the best of infrastructure. A little bit later, getting supper ready for the dog and cats, I saw the lights go on in my husband's garage and knew immediately what was going on. My husband was down on his knees saying a prayer to whomever he thinks is in charge of his world: *Dear keeper of my sanity: thank you for making me smart enough to not build a barn.*

The Rural Appreciation Society

1

A Farm Education

For someone who graduated from university with an English degree and a plan to teach high school, teaching the birds and the bees to elementary school children might seem off course. But really, it's no stranger than having a PhD in microbiology and driving cab or making cappuccinos while you search for a job in your field. If you want a job in your chosen field at all.

Who knew, even then, it was always about fields?

A year after I graduated from teachers' college, I covered a maternity leave at an outdoor education centre about an hour north of Toronto. The Etobicoke Field Studies Centre at the Claireville Conservation Area offered day programs to grades three to six students. The programs consisted of pond study, field study, wood study, and a farm visit; in the winter, there also was cross-country skiing and birdwatching. The teacher split the class in half and each group participated in two different programs, one in the morning and one after lunch.

For some students, a trip to Claireville once a year might be the only *natural* outdoors they ever experienced. The bus arrived at about 9:30 A.M. and left again at 2:00 P.M. Every so often, an entire class would scramble off the bus wearing sneakers and light jackets or sweatshirts better suited for walking along concrete sidewalks than tramping through woods or fields. Fortunately, the school kept extra rubber boots, gloves, and raincoats on hand.

I'd been at the field centre for nearly two months before I led my first solo tour of a local dairy farm. For some reason, it wasn't a popular choice among teachers; the woods, pond, and field studies fit better with the school curriculum. It was May before the "farm tour" box was ticked on the pre-visit information sheet. The school's other instructor ran me over to the farm for a quick introductory visit so I would be familiar with the milking barn, milk room, loafing shed, and the (very popular) calf barn.

"No problem," I told the instructor confidently when she said it was fairly straightforward. "I spent my summers on a dairy farm in Nova Scotia."

I might have overstated. The farm tour reminded me of hanging around Eldon Mundle's barns on Pugwash Point when I was twelve and thirteen, so naturally I felt like I knew something about farms and cows and milking. I completely disregarded that this initial visit to the local dairy farm was the first time I'd been near one in five years.

Nature always makes you walk in your own bullshit, however.

The day of my inaugural farm tour with twelve grade five students was warm and sunny. The big yellow bus bounced down the farm lane and let us out in front of a large, modern, grey steel barn. From inside, we heard mooing.

"Are those the cows, Miss?" one girl asked me.

I led them into the milking barn with its humid, pungent smell of bovine, milk, and manure.

"It stinks in here," a boy announced; the rest of the group concurred.

"What did you think a cow barn would smell like?" I smiled at the group of city kids while my eyes watered from the stench.

It was a job requirement, you see, to be enthusiastic about everything from manure to large spiders; I'd even managed to fake my way through catching a frog. Therefore, I trotted into the barn appearing completely confident in my ability to carry on despite feeling as woozy as the kids looked.

The farm tour took place only in the morning so the cows could remain in the barn after they'd been milked. I had just launched into my speech about the four stomachs when I felt a tug on the side of my shirt.

"Miss, what is that?" a student asked.

"What is what?" I looked around but saw nothing but black and white cows in stanchions chewing their cud.

"That," she said. "What is the cat eating?"

She pointed at the concrete floor running down the centre of the barn.

Oh, dear God in heaven.

The cat was—please, let it be licking, please don't let it be eating—what appeared to be a cow foetus.

"Um…I, um—"

At that moment, the farmer came out of the milk room on the other side of the barn. He pulled me to one side and quietly explained that the cows had been treated with antibiotics for a virus but a side effect of the medicine was spontaneous abortion. He walked back down the centre concrete strip and shooed the cat away.

I was twenty-four years old. I did not have a lot of experience with children, and I'd graduated from teachers' college trained for high school English. If this was nature's way of correcting my arrogance, I wasn't about to be cowed. I had spent a few weeks at Eldon's dairy farm; I could handle this. I explained to the students that in order to give milk, a cow must be pregnant and that cows only give milk when they have a baby inside them or have just given birth. Then I paraphrased the farmer's explanation without using the term "spontaneous abortion." I didn't want these kids blurting *that* out at suppertime.

Normally, the barn tour would be followed up with a trip to the milk room, but that meant walking past the foetus—which had now attracted the attention of two cats—so it was time to escape to the safer, less emotionally draining loafing shed.

The loafing shed was a three-walled building with a roof where the heifers hung out. They were free to roam but whenever humans appeared, they pressed their wet, pink noses through the fence. A few kids put their hands out to touch the side of a cow between the wooden slats but most jumped back with a squeal when a long, thick, slimy tongue appeared.

"Heifers are female cows that haven't had a baby yet," I explained.

I had to be careful: these kids were eleven and under and I wasn't interested in giving them a different kind of birds and bees spiel than the one they'd receive that afternoon during the field study. But nature was not about to let me off that easily.

A ruckus began inside the loafing shed and the heifers became agitated, pushing forward and backing up. I saw one heifer mounted on the back of another. It was no big deal, I've seen them do that, but the noise was too loud to talk over and the herd was pushing against the fence behind me.

"What's going on, Miss?" asked one girl.

The noise grew louder, the heifers more agitated.

"He's got his thing in her!" crowed a tall, pigtailed girl.

Now, I'm rather cow-like in my thinking processes: I like to chew on thoughts for a while before speaking, and remain placid in the face of chaos and confusion. But this was one of those moments where I wish were more chicken-like: squawking and flapping and running around in circles. Anything as a distraction.

If it hadn't been for the sweet little girl on my right, I might have provided a redacted explanation of what was happening and why. But then I had a fleeting vision of her sitting around the table that evening with her parents telling them what she learned at the outdoor education centre that afternoon, and I chickened out.

"Okay," I said, "we're getting these guys all worked up and we don't want to do that so let's move along to the best part of the tour. We're on our way to the calf barn and if you really want to see some cute cows, well, these are it!" I said, trying to convince myself as much as them. "Babies, just babies, hanging around in their pens, not doing anything but just being calves and waiting to be fed. All good here."

And for the first time that day, I was right. The calves cooperated and I was able to do my "isn't this great?" face while allowing a calf to suck on my fingers. The kids oohed and aahed and shrieked as one boy let a calf suck his entire hand. Suddenly, the bus reappeared and we returned to the centre for lunch.

I lay down on the cot in the supply room.

Here's the thing: when I was around this age, I saw things you only see on a farm. Things like very serious, very natural "birds and bees" proceedings that were far more explicit than what these little darlings saw with me on this farm tour. It didn't traumatize me and I didn't blurt out anything strange at the dinner table.

As I drove home from work that evening, thinking about the farm tour and wondering if I could have been just a little more sanguine about the whole visit, I remembered being twelve years old, just a year older than these students, and watching a mating process between horses at Eldon's farm.

Eldon didn't just have a dairy farm; for many years, he also raced horses and later, had a black stallion named Horton Hanover who provided stud service. We were staying in the old house that used to be on the farm property; a two-storey overlooking the barns and horse corral. One afternoon, my father called me to the upstairs window at the end of the hall.

For fifteen minutes, we stood watching Horton chase a brown mare around the corral, his engorged pink penis dragging through the dirt, the mare screeching every time he nipped her backside. Horton never did get his "thing in her" that day. They ran in circles around that corral until I got bored and wandered off to read.

Aside from that one afternoon, Horton usually didn't have to do much to get a mare pregnant. His stud service was much more civilized, keeping him at arm's length.

"C'mon," Eldon's older daughter, Sue, said to me one afternoon, "Dad's inseminating a mare."

Moments later, I stood in the horse barn, eyes as big and round as a bale of hay. Sue held the tail of a brown mare to one side while her father shoved his left arm shoulder-deep inside her. These were the days before Eldon donned a long plastic glove. This could have been the moment I learned to appear totally unfazed by things—*his entire arm is up the back end of that horse!*—and I was doing all right with that, keeping my mouth closed and controlling the urge to run around squawking and flapping my arms, until Eldon said, "I forgot to take off my wedding ring."

As much as I wanted to claim a deep connection to farm life and be as cool and confident around the farm animals as my friend Sue, if you haven't grown up around this stuff, you're just a city girl stepping in piles of manure with your mouth hanging open.

2

Ghosts in Our Machines

⸺ · ·· ⸺

To be a farmer—to own a few hundred acres for livestock and feed, to remain true to the community in which you were raised, and to remain small and traditional—means wondering what will happen to this farm started by your father because none of your children see any point in taking it over. It means having an unlimited supply of optimism and faith. Not only when it comes to the weather, but also when it comes to the world. You need to believe that enough of the world remembers where food comes from, respects the hard work and long hours that go into producing it, and understands what is lost every time a farm closes its barn doors or rolls up its hayfields.

I wasn't thinking about any of this when we showed up at the Antique Farm Show in Lorneville, Nova Scotia, one Saturday afternoon in July. I wanted to support some new friends but at the same time, after seven years in rural Nova Scotia, I felt it was time I experienced one of these shows. As a newspaper reporter and a newbie country girl, it seemed like the right thing to do.

If I'd known that there was so much more to a farm show than tractors and tools, I would have gone years ago. With the smell of hay in the air, antique tractors were lined up neatly in the freshly mowed field and an eclectic assortment of stationary engines, saws, mowers, and balers (I had to ask my husband what was what) sat on display. Inside a mobile, working replica of a blacksmith's shop, Jerry Thompson stooped over a hot forge, demonstrating how common items like nails, hooks, and horseshoes used to be made. Under a huge white tent, the local band, Pic 'n' Grin, belted out familiar country and gospel songs. As the Sunrise 4-H Club fired up their barbecue, people began lining up at the canteen, anticipating a slice or two of the pies made by the ladies of the local United Church. Others worked up an appetite by climbing aboard the pickup-drawn wagon for a tour of Francis Verstraten's award-winning woodlot. I thought it was a great crowd for a tractor show.

"I wish I'd come to one of these shows before," I said to the co-host Polly Verstraten, my mouth full of a delicious 4-H–cooked hamburger. "This is so much fun."

"This is our last one," Polly told me. "After fifteen years, we're done."

There weren't enough slices of pie to console me, but Polly's news made the reporter in me grateful I'd made it to this final show: every loss in the farming community must be documented. These stories may not stop the decline, but they deserve to be told; every loss in a farming community is a loss for the global community.

"Exhibitor interest is waning," Polly told me, "and that's the whole reason behind the show, to bring the machinery and people together. Everything runs in cycles and this has kind of run its cycle. It's so busy for everyone everywhere. There are too many pulls on people's attention."

I can't help but think of the trickle-down effect when this show, or any show like it, shuts down: The ladies selling pies lose a fundraiser for their rural church. The 4-H group loses one of their main sources of funding. A generation loses the chance to listen to a live performance of their favourite music.

Fifteen years of hosting this show for the North Shore Antique Tractor and Engine Club is significant considering the onus of preparation and presentation on the Verstratens (who, until 2009, ran a working dairy farm). Polly's husband, Francis—a lifelong farmer and antique tractors and tools enthusiast—joined the club in the mid-1990s because he wanted to preserve farm history by buying old equipment from closed-down farms.

"We bought this farm from my parents in 1989," Polly explained about the farm in Lorneville overlooking the Amherst Shore and Northumberland Strait. "Francis is from Collingwood [a community fifty kilometres south on the other side of the TransCanada Highway] and he didn't know a lot of people around here so he got into the habit of inviting some of the old farmers in once a week or so for an evening. He called it his 'pioneer club,'" Polly chuckled. "He'd haul an old piece of equipment out of the barn, they'd talk about it, come in for tea and cookies, and then they'd start telling stories about who used to farm here, who used to work together, about going across the ice in wintertime in their trucks to Port Elgin to get whatever came in on the train. Francis loved that rural history."

Making his commitment to preserving history a little more formal, Francis joined the North Shore Antique Tractor and Engine Club: a group that loved old farm equipment and collecting, remembering, and swapping stories. While Francis didn't restore any of the old farm equipment he bought, one man in the club had enough skill to get some of the pieces working so they could, as Polly put it, "play with them." As membership and the collection of antique tractors grew, the club decided to host a show and provide demos for the general public.

"We volunteered to host the show because we had the space and we started the first one [in 1999] in the farmyard," Polly laughed. "The first couple of years it was up in the yard because we have a circular driveway so there was a natural circuit between the barns and the buildings and the cottage. We'd get about a hundred people including exhibitors. It started to grow year after year—people would arrive from as far away as Halifax and the north shore of New Brunswick—so we decided to expand it down into the field."

When the Verstratens sold their cows and quota in 2009, they cleared out the barn. At that year's farm show, the 4-H canteen and church ladies set up shop inside, selling juicy hamburgers and hot-dogs and a wide selection of homemade pies. Vacating the barn also created an empty space that allowed Francis to conserve those tangibles of rural history.

"It broke his heart to look around the countryside and see all the old farms that were put aside," Polly said. "People had stopped working them, the fields were growing up, and the barns were falling down. Francis knew there was stuff in those barns that people used and loved. So people would come to the show to see their stuff—they would come to see the old tractors that we had bought."

Turns out, what I thought was just a bunch of ol' timers leaning on antique tractors and talking about the good ol' days is merely a fraction of a farm show. They are indeed telling stories, but those stories are part of the industrial history of this community. And that history is important.

"If we don't listen now and if we don't gather the stories, they're gone," Polly said. "Those people, when they pass, that information and all the stuff that happened is gone with them. The more of them that are gone, the farther we get from the roots of our country and our lives, how we are fed, how a community grows, how those things happen." Polly's voice became impassioned. "We need to keep reminding people that they get their food from the grocery store but this is where it started, this is how your family got here—through the hard work of these people."

People like Polly and Francis.

Francis's parents emigrated from Holland after the Second World War and although they started out in Ontario, they eventually came to Nova Scotia and settled on a farm in Collingwood. When their father fell ill, Francis and his brother took over the family farm. Some time in the early eighties, Francis Verstraten laid eyes on Polly Siddall at a dance in Collingwood (at the time, Polly was a neonatal nurse in Halifax but had gone to the dance with the man she was dating). A few years later, they married and moved to her parents' dairy farm on the Amherst Shore.

"Our kids are the sixth generation on this farm," Polly said. "It's been in the family since 1820."

But their three children have all chosen non-farming careers. When Francis and Polly decided to move on from dairy and simply do cash crops along with a woodlot, they were facing reality, no longer following their hearts.

"We hit a stage where we either had to throw a bunch more money in, knowing the kids weren't going to come back, or let the cows and quota go and get out from under our debt but still have work to do," explained Polly. "It's more difficult to sell a going operation with dairy farms getting bigger, not smaller.

"So we're semi-retired. We're still keeping our hand in, but with cattle you have to be around and Francis likes to travel."

What amazes me is the kernel of hope I hear when she talks about the future; Polly is keeping a firm grip on one last dangling thread of optimism. That trait that has likely kept farmers going long after common sense—and perhaps the bank manager—suggested it was time to cut loose.

"We haven't sold any land so if farming should take a turn around and the kids want to come back, that whole infrastructure is still there," Polly admitted.

Infrastructure. Such a vague and corporate word for the rural history that lies fallow in those fields, waiting for another generation: another bunch of ol' timers to turn it over and share it with the world.

3

A Walk in the Woods

In the early years of my marriage to a Nova Scotia country boy, he left for work shortly after 6:00 A.M. and often wasn't home until 6:00 P.M. As an introvert, reader, and writer, this didn't bother me: I liked having the house to myself all day, and I was particularly fond of starting my day alone.

Although I married for love, not property, I quickly learned there's nothing nicer than having land of one's own to wander around, especially in the early morning when the human world has not quite stirred to life.

I am fortunate to have fallen in love with a man who owns seventy-two acres of fields, woods, open sky, and leafy canopy. Born and raised in this river valley, he knows by heart the land I'm still mapping with my feet, eyes, and soul. Slowly, every day, I am carving my own trail through his land: under the osprey nest, through the spruce plantation, along the top of the field, and into the woods. The frozen field crunches under my boots as the dog and I enter the stillness of the plantation. This fourteen-acre woodlot my husband planted in 1997 provides a refuge from the wind no matter which direction it's blowing from.

The land here is soft and wet, the trail winding and riddled with potential water holes, so I have to watch where I'm walking. A distinctive call pierces the air this morning and I whip my head up to find the source. A pileated woodpecker is hopping up a limb in a dead tree. Rather than being startled by the appearance of the dog and me, it simply sits, grooming, as I pause to watch. From the distance, I hear a knocking and to this, the pileated woodpecker reacts: it sits up straight and listens. The knocking sounds again and—swoosh—the bird flits from the branch with a flash of its wide, white under-wings. Off to find its friend and perhaps suggest breakfast at the dead pine at the top of the field.

When I reach the point where the woods push up against the edges of the old, unimproved road, I stand still for a moment. The field sprawls to my right, undulating towards the spruce plantation, while the woods on my left crackle with quiet. There is our red-sided house in the distance and greyish clouds billowing behind the treeline, promising flurries this afternoon. A croaking breaks the silence as a pair of ravens flies overhead, the *whup-whup* of their black wings carrying through the cold air. As the sound fades, we continue on up the old road and into the woods.

In her poem "How I Go to the Woods," Mary Oliver writes:

Ordinarily, I go to the woods alone,
with not a single friend,
for they are all
smilers and talkers and therefore unsuitable.

These lines drift through my mind as I trudge behind the dog, her nose to the ground, through the rest of the plantation. The dog loves our walks because I pay no attention to her; she is free to follow the trail of rabbit tracks into the poplar trees without my sharp voice spoiling the scent.

Coming to live on this land after thirty-six years in the city was like piling all my suppressed ideas inside the fire pit in the yard and lighting a match: I became a bonfire of creativity. All I wanted to do was write. Walk, write, write some more, and then walk again. Every so often, I would come across an essay praising the combination of writing, dogs, and walking. It's a logical trinity: if you have a dog, you walk. If you write, you walk. An unspeaking dog intent on smells and a pondering walker intent on inner thoughts make natural companions in the woods. Some humans do not understand the pleasure of being alone but dogs do. The dog will disappear into the woods with me. "When I am alone I can become invisible," Oliver writes.

Yet on these acres, I am never alone. I am surrounded by creatures both domesticated and wild: dogs, cats, a flock of chickens, and a trio of rabbits; the colourful crowds at the bird feeders, ospreys, eagles, and a lone cock pheasant; mice, foxes, a black bear, and the graceful white-tailed deer who criss-cross the field. Once, a pair of mainland moose tromped across the field, he following she. It was a rare and mesmerizing sight. For weeks following the sight, I thought I could hear them crashing through the trees when they sensed the dog and me deep in the woods, but I never saw them again.

At night, we hear coyotes howling from across the river where the woods are thicker and there are fewer homes. I have only seen a coyote in the woods behind our place once, far beyond our property line before it was clear-cut. A long flash of light grey caught my eye, and I saw a coyote, lean and long-legged. It stared at me for a moment then loped away, disappearing quickly. So, for Valentine's Day a few years ago, my husband gave me a .22 rifle. He thinks his former city girl needs to know how to shoot a gun.

"You can carry this when you walk in the woods in case you meet some coyotes," he said, helpfully.

When I was living in Vancouver and driving to work at four in the morning, I encountered two coyotes trotting down the middle of Main Street. I drove behind them slowly, willing them to get out of the way. The closer one stopped suddenly and I braked. It turned to look at me and I remember being glad my doors were locked. The streetwise look and unhurried gait of those two inner-city creatures assured me I was on their turf.

Whose turf are these woods? What if coyotes attack my dog? The questions conjure a picture in my mind: me driving a sharp stick into the neck of the coyote that has my dog by the throat. Would I have the strength to do that? Arms raised above my head, stick pointed downwards, a roar coming out of my mouth. How strong is my protective instinct? How much rage is stored in me for moments such as these? And yet, my valentine gift remains locked in its case, never loaded and never fired. I go to the woods for peace, so I go in peace.

I know a woman who is psychic; she can hear people's thoughts and sees images associated with them but uses her gift only with animals (she finds humans too resistant to her information). She once told me a story about walking in the woods in northern Ontario and meeting a bear. She held a conversation with the bear, thinking her thoughts and receiving his communication as a voice in her head.

"Whoa, you stink," Kim said as soon as she came upon him.

To that, the bear apparently replied, "You don't smell so good to me, either."

The bear did not threaten her, she said, and she did not feel afraid. Since hearing that story, I've walked in the woods with a pure heart. If I come face-to-face with one of the black bears who roam our area, I want it to know I am a friend. I also know that you back away from a black bear, don't run, and drop as many items of clothing as you can as a distraction.

"The day I arrive home naked," I said to my husband, "you'll know I met a bear in the woods."

Mary Oliver does not write about walking backwards or naked in "How I Go to the Woods," but she does mention not wanting to be "witnessed talking to the catbirds or hugging the old black oak tree/I have my way of praying, as you no doubt have yours." I like to think if I were to meet a bear in the woods, I would put my hands in prayer position in front of my chest and bow slightly, like we do at the end of a yoga class. This gesture serves to communicate *my heart acknowledges your heart.* Hopefully it would work.

"If you have ever gone to the woods with me," writes Mary Oliver in her final stanza, "I must love you very much."

The dog walks on, wandering off the unimproved road to the edge of the woods where she unintentionally flushes a partridge out of the brush.

"Oh!" I exclaim to the woods, startled, my breath a puff of white in the cold air. Like love encountered unexpectedly, it makes my heart beat faster and I feel more alive than I've ever felt before...even if I am alone in the woods.

4

The Rural Wavelength

*I*f you have lived most of your life in the city or outside of the Maritimes, a phenomenon that occurs in rural Nova Scotia—and, I'm sure, rural New Brunswick and Prince Edward Island—can be a bit disconcerting. If you are not born with this behaviour genetically implanted in your DNA—which is to say, if you were not conceived by Maritimers and born with red soil between your toes—it is quite possible you can never fully embrace this aspect of rural life.

Let's go back to May 2002. After five years of living in Vancouver, I'd just arrived with my parents at their summer home on Pugwash Point. It had been ten years since my last visit to Nova Scotia and in that time, the closest I'd come to rural life was working at an outdoor education centre north of Toronto. Getting settled into the old house on the hill at the first of the season required several trips into the village for supplies, which meant driving by the house of our nearest neighbour. On this particular day, Gary was working in his yard and every time my mother and I drove by, he waved. Every time, Mum waved back.

After driving by his house on our second trip into the village, I finally asked, "Do we have to wave *every* time we drive by?"

"Yes," my mother answered.

I've been traumatized ever since.

For someone who grew up with the rule, "Your father owns a business in this town so your behaviour in public affects him," living in big cities where no one knew me was a lovely freedom from the threat of nosy neighbours and tattletales. I didn't have to worry about paying attention to the cars going by. If I wanted to ignore people, I could. What I did was nobody's business. (Granted, in my first year of university, before I realized I was so near-sighted I should be wearing my glasses full-time, a good friend did wonder why I couldn't see him walking down the sidewalk toward me: "I've been waving at you," he said.)

Fast-forward four years from my return to the Point: Gary set me up on a blind date with a friend of his from work. Dwayne picked me up from the house and drove us to Springhill for supper. During that forty-minute drive, he waved at *every* vehicle we passed. I wasn't nervous about a date with a man I barely knew but I was freaked out by the fact he seemed to know every single person in this part of the county. What had I gotten myself into?

We all know the answer to that.

Although living here permanently hasn't reduced my anxiety about the expectation of waving to everyone (second only to my anxiety about the requirement of opening every conversation with some insightful comment about the weather), it has allowed me to make a study of it. As far as I can make out, there are three distinct waves that make up this Maritime phenomenon, as extrapolated from my (decidedly unscientific) research conducted in Cumberland County.

Wave Number One: the "Gary Wave"

This is the most physically demanding of all the waves and shouldn't be attempted by people with heart conditions (please check with your physician). The Gary Wave involves throwing both arms up into the air and flinging them side to side.

Now, upon seeing someone executing this wave properly, you may assume he or she is in some kind of distress. If Gary were up to his waist in water, you'd assume he was drowning. But since Gary is standing in his driveway with a big smile on his face, you realize he is waving (and possibly practicing some dance moves at the same time). The good thing is you are driving and not expected to respond with the same amount of enthusiasm or exertion. You only need Wave Number Two.

Wave Number Two: the "Dwayne Wave"

This is the most common wave. I was introduced to this one on that first date with my future husband and, as far as I can tell, it is used exclusively by men driving pickup trucks. It involves lifting of two fingers—specifically, the forefinger and middle finger—from the steering wheel, just barely an inch, holding for a brief moment then laying them back down. This wave is repeated as often as necessary and results in a pretty good workout for those fingers.

My observations have revealed that men tend to identify vehicles rather than drivers, which may explain why so many men wave at me when I'm driving my husband's truck. "Everyone thinks you're stuck up today because you didn't wave at anyone," I have to advise him when I return home.

Wave Number Three: the "Nicole Wave"

This wave is popular among women. Properly executed, it suggests the driver is squealing with excitement—"Omigawd, hi, hi, hi!"—as she waves. There is a particular technique for this wave, which could be why men eschew it. As the hand releases its grip on the steering wheel completely, the wrist flings back and up, and the hand waves back and forth vigorously. It is a very friendly and enthusiastic wave, and could be considered a version of the Gary Wave toned down for the safe operation of a motor vehicle.

On the other hand, I must acknowledge many women don't use any sort of wave at all; my unscientific study suggests men wave at every vehicle because it looks like so-and-so's, whereas women don't wave unless they are *sure* and often the car is past before they realize they knew the driver. Who knew waving was so complicated?

Some people take waving very seriously: they want to receive as much as they give. My friend Jane once had this conversation with a woman who said she waves at Jane every time she sees her walking her dog:

"But you don't wave back," the woman admonished.

"I have a hard time seeing people behind the windshield," Jane replied.

"But you know it's my car, don't you?"

Although she couldn't believe she was actually having this conversation, Jane replied with uncharacteristic patience, "No, I don't identify people by their vehicles."

(What she really wanted to say was, "I don't give a rat's ass what kind of car you drive.")

"Oh, well, then, I'll toot when I drive by so you know it's me and can wave back," the woman told Jane and went on her way, happy to have solved the problem and thereby adding a fourth wave: the Toot.

The "Toot"

The Toot, although technically not a wave, occurs when someone driving by a pedestrian uses his or her horn. It is accompanied by a wave. Hearing the Toot means you know the person very well (unless you are in the city; then it simply means you are about to get run over in a crosswalk) and can wave without even looking at the vehicle.

The Toot is usually administered gently unless you are a man by the name of Randy Smith; in that case, you lay on your truck horn as soon as you are alongside me as I'm walking the dog so I jump a metre off the ground and land headfirst in the ditch. That's one way of getting a wave out of me, I suppose: waving frantically for help. Let's call that wave the Randy; its distinctive characteristic is a certain finger pointing straight to the sky.

All joking aside, waving must be how Maritimers got their reputation for being so friendly (that, combined with the long story in response to the question, "Hi, how are you?"). It doesn't bother Maritimers at all to wave at people they don't know. Some wave because they think they know the truck; others, who live in *really* small areas, simply wave at every vehicle because the odds are they do know them. If they don't, well, one has to be friendly to visitors, after all.

I knew I'd taken a step into this dark side when my mother and I were driving through Oxford one afternoon and I waved at someone because I thought I knew the vehicle. Of course, I was wrong—which is why I never wave; I don't know anybody—but it turns out the car was from Ontario. I know from my past life as a vacationer that waving freaks out visitors. That person from Ontario could have spent the rest of his or her vacation trying to figure out who they knew in Cumberland County, Nova Scotia, because someone waved at them.

I've come to recognize waving as friendliness; an acknowledgement of my predictable presence as the dog and I walk along the road. Now, I automatically return the wave even if I have no idea who is behind it. Mostly because the man driving the brown pickup with two other people crammed into the front seat waves at me every morning and I still don't know who he is. This is what I love about rural life: if you're here, you're part of the wave. You might as well ride it.

5

Learning to Drive, Country Style

I once wore a nightgown to a sleepover in a hayloft. There. I've admitted it: my life's deepest embarrassment. This was the other big reason I was disqualified me from ever becoming a "real" farm girl (the first being I didn't grow up on a farm).

It was some time in the eighties, during one of our August vacations on Pugwash Point. We no longer stayed at Garth and Dorothy's cabin on the back shore of the Mundles' dairy farm; we now spent our holidays right on the farm in MacCrae House, the huge, old home that once dominated the farm property and overlooked Pugwash Harbour.

By the time we started staying at the old house at the farm, I was twelve years old and no longer wanted to go with my parents on their endless road trips. I wanted to spend my days hanging out on the farm, doing cool farm things with my friend Sue, who was a year older. To me, the visitor from Ontario, Sue was clever and confident, walking behind cows without fear of their switching tails, helping lug cans full of warm milk to the tank, unfazed by the manure that was everywhere, including her shoes and jeans. It didn't upset her a bit; it was part of being an honest-to-goodness farm girl.

My memories of Sue and I are frozen in time: it will always be summer and we will always be teenage girls. I will always be Sue's sidekick as she drives the pickup truck over the fields to deliver juice to the boys haying in the hot August sun, or training the best mare for the sulky races in Truro. I am always trailing along as she wades the other horses in the ocean to ease their sores, or holds bottles of milk for the newborn calves.

Sue's simple acceptance of me, eager and clumsy and perhaps even at times a nuisance, made me feel like her *friend*. Her daily chores were all new experiences for me but my lack of knowledge made me shy about asking to help. I envied Sue having her own horse, her ease around the cows, her single-mindedness about her life—once a farm girl, always a farm girl—even as an adolescent. As she went about her business, I trailed along behind, happy enough to be in her universe. Sue wasn't the country bumpkin; I was the clueless city girl.

The summer I was twelve was the summer of my first kiss. Every evening after supper, I followed Sue to the barn where we hung out with Pat, who milked the cows every morning and evening with one of his sons. One evening, his son and I snuck off to the horse barn and the lasting impression of our kisses is the smell of manure.

It was also the summer of the sleepover. I honestly don't know how to describe it accurately. Fiasco? Disaster? It's not hyperbole, however, when I say it's my life's greatest embarrassment, (and that's saying something considering some of the men I've dated). Maybe, though, it's no longer embarrassment that burdens me, but regret.

Far more than my first kiss, Sue's casual invitation to sleep in the hayloft of the horse barn would turn out to be a pivotal moment in my life. The day progressed as normal and once it was dark, I slipped inside our house to brush my teeth and use the bathroom then met up with Sue to head to the horse barn.

I could have been cool and slept in my clothes just like she did, but I had no experience with sleeping in a hayloft or a tent or anything that wasn't a bed with sheets and blankets. I was completely unaccustomed to any situation where you didn't, mustn't, keep your usual bedtime routine. Although I don't remember bringing a bag with me, when the time came to get into our sleeping bags, I changed out of my jeans and sweatshirt and into a full-length cotton nightgown.

I will never forget the way the energy in that warm, dusty hayloft altered as Sue realized what I was doing. Her reaction wasn't as obvious as a frown or a joke; she didn't say a word. Perhaps she turned away and I caught a wry smile on her face but I don't remember specifically. I just felt the subtle change in our status with the sixth sense any young girl has when it comes to social situations. Any potential I had as her protégé, her trusted confidante, fizzled in that moment: I had flubbed. I knew I had lost any cool quotient that came with being the vacationing friend from Ontario.

Fortunately, Sue was not mean-spirited and throughout the following summers, before I stopped going east once I'd started university, she remained my friend. If I could no longer be her protégé, at least I could become her partner in crime. One crime, the only illegal act I've committed in my life.

Hanging out with Sue and enjoying the freedom that came with living on a farm (and our parents trusting that we were acting safely and sensibly) infused me with a greater willingness to do whatever Sue did. Especially since I knew I had to make up for the nightgown-in-the-hayloft *faux pas*. Looking back, I have no idea what Sue was thinking; perhaps this was as close as she would get to being a "mean girl" to the clueless friend from Ontario. It seemed like a good idea at the time.

Our crime spree started when Sue discovered her older brother's brand new, shiny, red Trans Am parked in the driveway.

"Let's go to the racetrack," Sue said. "You can drive."

This might have been another test for me to fail, but given my well-documented lack of knowledge about country living, there was no reason for Sue to think I could drive a bicycle, let alone a car. Did I mention it was brand new?

Of course, as the farm girl, she'd been driving the tractor since she was eight years old. It must have seemed inconceivable to her, already sixteen and able to drive any vehicle, that a fifteen-year-old wouldn't know how to drive a car. Maybe she wasn't being mean; maybe she was trying to educate me. She may have wanted to start with the farm pickup.

What amazes me to this day is that I hopped into the driver's seat fully prepared to drive that vehicle. Fully prepared in terms of nerve (and completely uncharacteristic boldness) but also in terms of knowing what to do once I'd snapped on the seatbelt.

Which I didn't.

I could turn on the ignition, I could put the car into gear (it was automatic), and I knew to put both hands on the steering wheel. After that, it was a crapshoot. In Paul's brand new sports car.

And yet, Sue wasn't kidding: I put her brother's car into drive and we sallied forth. How we got out of the farmyard with no one seeing us is beyond me—our parents must have been away on one of their road trips that day—but off we went down the driveway and onto the paved road in front of the farm. This wasn't the road to the racetrack, however: to get there, we'd have to leave the dead-end Point Road and drive several kilometers through the village of Pugwash.

You know how in every movie chase scene, the cars careen through a major intersection on a red light, dodging dozens of cars, all of which crash into each other but leave the main characters' vehicle unscathed? Well, we weren't being chased but we managed to careen through a major intersection. Luckily for us, the main intersection of Church and Durham Streets rarely saw a dozen cars back then; it really didn't need a stop sign, let alone traffic lights.

When we eventually did come to the stop sign, calling what I did a "rolling stop" would be generous and totally inaccurate. When I swung left around that corner without even slowing down (I didn't know how to take my right foot off the gas and pump the brakes), my eyes may or may not have been open. I simply turned the corner and drove through the east end of the village, around a sharp corner, and then swung left again onto the road that led to the racetrack.

When we finally pulled up alongside the stables, I screeched to a stop with a seatbelt-freezing jolt, a laugh, and a rush of adrenaline. *Holy crap, we made it! And I drove a car!*

Technically, I can't say I learned to drive in Nova Scotia but like so many other firsts in my life, the first time I drove a car was in Nova Scotia—with the true farm girl riding shotgun.

When I think back to those summers when we stayed at MacCrae House, the memories are as clear as the blue, mid-August sky and as sparkling as end-of-summer sun dancing on the waves in the Pugwash Harbour. The passage of time has simplified the details but not the feelings, or the longings. I think I am still that fifteen-year-old girl from Ontario with her novels and her notebook and her camera, spending her mornings reading on the antique fainting couch in the living room, her afternoons in the barn with the cows and the horses, and her nights looking at the stars above the one place on earth where no one cares that she doesn't quite fit in.

I have come to accept that I will never be a farm girl. I don't possess Sue's confidence or skill with livestock, but I can thank her for laying the necessary foundation for me to become a country girl. Those idyllic summers spent trailing after Sue taught me how to be observant, how to be adventurous, how to kiss a Nova Scotia country boy, and—most importantly—what not to bring to a sleepover in a hayloft.

6

Muslims in the Maritimes

The tea Sam Mohamad pours into white mugs is his own creation: a mix of green tea and the dried blossoms from a Russian olive tree growing in the ditch by his home near Pugwash.

"You probably never see it," says the fifty-two-year-old father of four. "Every year when the blossoms come, I pick some and dry them because we have those trees back home."

Russian olive trees, despite the name, are native to Lebanon, the country Sam left at the age of twenty-two. It was 1988, only a few months after he'd married Alia Kamareddine in their village of Mechmech, Akkar, in the mountains of Lebanon.

"My family had moved down from the mountains to live by the sea but we kept in touch. One day I was walking in Mechmech and Alia was in her parents' grocery store. That was the first time I met her."

Alia's father had died a couple of years earlier so she was at the store, helping her older brother.

"I was working when Sam came in. We looked at each other and fell in love," Alia says.

Their Muslim faith dictated that the pair couldn't date, so Sam had to get someone to ask Alia if she liked him. As it turns out, that was the easy part; Alia's mother had other plans for her daughter.

"Once I met Sam, I wanted him and when he asked me to marry him, I said yes. He was a handsome man back then," she laughs. "When I said yes, his family came to ask for my hand and my mother said no. She said I was too young and that I had to finish my education."

Alia obeyed until her sister-in-law, who happened to be Sam's cousin, convinced her mother to let Alia get married. Sam already had begun the process of applying to immigrate to Canada when he met Alia, but since both of them had grown up during the civil war that raged in Lebanon from 1975 to 1990, the soon-to-be-married couple agreed they wanted a safer place to live, work, and raise a family.

"With my luck, we got married and three days later, I got my visa," Sam says. "I had no choice; I left. It was very sad to leave my wife."

When Sam and his two friends arrived in Toronto, they were put on an eastbound train to join one of Sam's brothers who was already in Nova Scotia.

"We couldn't find work in Halifax," Sam remembers, "so we went to Wolfville where my brother was making pizzas. Our first job was picking apples."

It wasn't the work that was challenging—he had no problem picking apples—the hard work was communicating. Sam spoke no English and had to communicate everything through rudimentary sign language.

"My real name is Hussein," Sam confides. "People we worked with found it hard to call me by my real name. They kept saying 'Sein' so that was close to Sam. It seems everybody who came from back home, they picked a nickname for right away."

All three of the Mohamad brothers created "Canadian names" for themselves after they arrived from Lebanon; only within the family do they use their birth names. Alia and his brothers call him Hussein but the rest of the community knows him as Sam.

Back home in Lebanon, Alia was enjoying the freedom that comes with being a married woman with a husband in Canada: "No husband to tell me what to do, no mother to tell me. That was the life," she recalls with a smile.

In the end, she couldn't get a visa to Canada so eleven months after marrying Sam, she travelled to the United States as a refugee. She flew with her new brother-in-law, Joe, (who now lives in Pugwash) to Chicago, Illinois, then to Bangor, Maine, where a friend of Sam's picked them up; Sam couldn't make the trip because as a landed immigrant, he couldn't leave Canada. The friend brought Alia and Joe to St. Stephen, New Brunswick, where Sam was waiting. They applied for refugee status and were accepted into Canada.

"I was just young," Alia says of her eighteen-year-old self. "I didn't care, there was no worry. Now I think back. How did I do that? So fearless."

After another year of picking apples in the valley and working in a pizzeria in Wolfville, Sam and Alia had saved enough to buy a restaurant in Cole Harbour and start their family.

With no family to help, they struggled after their first child was born. They both worked in the restaurant and lived in the basement until they could buy a house. The only English words Alia knew were "thank you."

"I was five months here and we had our own business and I didn't speak any English," Alia says. "Every time a customer come in, I said, 'Can you write that for me?' I didn't even know the alphabet. I'd answer the phone and say, 'Hello, Pasta House,' and she'd give me an address and she had to spell it for me. It was so hard. God knows where Sam used to go on delivery," she laughs.

"It was hard," Sam agrees, "but that's how we learned: talking to people. We survived. We did good. Coming here, no English, starting from zero. The Syrian refugees, they are lucky. They have people to help them, to translate for them."

It was the kindness of one stranger, who became a friend, which Alia still holds as a cherished memory.

"Linda came into the restaurant when I was pregnant. I didn't speak any English. She thought of me as this poor Lebanese girl;

she thought I was cute because I am little. She bought pizza from me then the next day, she brought me a baby gift. How nice was that when she didn't know me at all. I never forgot that gift. You know, I still have it."

In 1994, Sam and Alia sold their business and went back to Lebanon to visit their families. In the meantime, Sam's brother, Joe, decided to sell his pizza business in Pugwash and he offered it first to Sam and Alia upon their return to Canada. Sam says it was a relief to move out of the city where there was so much competition and little left over after paying the bills.

They say it didn't seem to matter to their new neighbours or customers that they were Lebanese Muslims.

"There were a couple of kids who picked on my kids at school but the principal fixed that," says Sam. "We really felt very comfortable. Small town, good place to raise our kids. We stayed five years in Dartmouth and our neighbour, we don't know his name."

They sold the Pugwash business a couple of years ago and currently run a pizzeria in Oxford where, once a month, Alia offers up a traditional Lebanese meal featuring kebabs, rice, tabbouleh, stuffed grape leaves, and falafel with hummus. If she offers dessert, it's her version of baklava: walnuts and honey rolled in puff pastry instead of cut into squares.

At home, Alia and her family eat the traditional foods of Lebanon, made the way she learned as a teenager, including homemade yogurt (laban) and her favourite dish, fatteh, which is baked pita bread topped with chicken or chickpeas, yogurt, and sliced almonds or pine nuts. The most common ingredients she cooks with are olive oil, garlic, and lemon, while the food is flavoured with mint, oregano, rosemary, pepper, and sumac, which a sister-in-law sends over from Lebanon. With Sam's special tea, Alia serves homemade turnovers filled with cheese.

Other traditions have been harder to maintain. Raising three boys and one girl in a different, non-Muslim culture has been as big a challenge as working without knowing the language.

"It's hard because our religion doesn't let us have boyfriend and girlfriend," Sam explains. "It's hard for us to keep them on track. They want to do like their friends."

After nearly thirty years, several visits to Lebanon, and one failed attempt to resettle in Australia with some of Alia's siblings, Sam and his wife have no regrets about moving to Canada and settling in rural Nova Scotia.

"When we came here, it was a big test and we came through it," Sam says. "Lots of people have relatives here and they get lots of help. We didn't have anybody. The only thing that upset me was not having family here. I would have gone to the community college and got a good job. That's one thing—I should have went to school."

Since Alia didn't finish high school, she insists her daughter, Zaynah, still in high school, will get a good education.

"Nowadays, a woman has to be well educated so she can depend on herself, not on her husband," says Alia. "I am my own boss because I work and earn money." Zaynah already has indicated she'd like to be a doctor or pharmacist.

What saddens Alia is how difficult it was to maintain her native language with her children; they understand Arabic but don't speak it very well.

"They spend six hours at school and they do their homework in English. Sam and I, we're working and have no time to sit down and teach them. How Wassim and Khoder learned it, I paid lots of money for a special teacher when we went to Australia for a year and a half."

That was when the two oldest boys, now in their twenties, were in high school. Alia missed her family, many of whom had emigrated from Lebanon to Australia after her mother died, and was tired of winter in Canada. In the end, though, their children missed their Canadian friends.

When asked about Wassim, the oldest and newly married to a young woman from Lebanon, Sam's face breaks into a wide grin. "He went to university to become a mining engineer. I'm so proud," he says. "Khoder didn't go to university but I said if you don't go to university, at least go to college to get a good job. You can't work for minimum wage and survive."

Neither Sam nor Alia want their children to follow in the family business.

"I don't want to see them work seven days a week for twenty-five years," he says. "We're really tired out."

Sipping her husband's tea, Alia nods in agreement. "When the kids are out of the house, I want to go to Australia in the winter."

7

What Future Does a Tree Have?

The spirit world is connected to the world of breathing creatures.
An old man can't be too happy about his afterlife.
If his soul should choose a tree after it has left his body,
what will become of it?
What future does a tree have nowadays?

—Chief Dan George

The one great sorrow of my life in rural Nova Scotia is the death of trees. The Department of Natural Resources, the woods associations, and the loggers can say what they like about sustainability, the economy, and jobs, but I live with the reality of this province's head-in-the-sand approach to forestry. Beside our property—land my husband's father gave him in the late 1970s—runs an unmaintained government road. Last used as a real road over fifty years ago, it's now merely a track that runs through several hundred acres of lovely, quiet woods. There's a tricky sinkhole halfway through and if you don't know where it is, you risk losing your four-wheeler in it. Otherwise, though, it's a lovely spot to walk, ride, and explore.

The problem with this unimproved road is it still allows easy access to the woods; its abandonment also seems to imply that logging operations will have no impact. No impact? Since 2009, there have been three separate logging operations behind our house. Every activity we used to enjoy in those woods, from walking to snowshoeing to four-wheeling, has been impacted by those cuts. When I first moved here, those woods made my heart sing with the rightness of finding the space in which I belong, in which I could put down roots.

It was quite a shock, then, to listen and watch as non-metaphorical roots were yanked out of the ground, severed from the trunk, and left to rot amid the branchy bones flung on the ground.

The first operation by a local company was deep in the woods. One might think this would have no impact on us, but it destroyed the path to the open spot on the north side of the Ducks Unlimited pond where my husband and I had been enjoying small bonfires and mugs of tea from a thermos since the day after I'd moved in. After the machines left, we drove out to investigate. The new landscape disoriented me. Without the familiar markers of the trees—this is where that copse of birch was, this is where those pines trees stood at the opening to our path—the landscape was unrecognizable. It was made worse by the remains of the devastation, tops and bottoms of the trees left behind like collateral damage. The only consolation was that, in losing their woods, the deer gained treetops to feed on for the rest of winter.

Two years later, my husband broke the news to me again: one of the Maritimes' main logging companies was going to cut down the woods it owned; woods even closer to our home this time, and within my regular dog-walking range.

A week later, just before six o'clock in the morning, the rumble of a large truck slowing down in front of our house jerked me awake.

I knew what that braking sound heralded: I had been in denial, but now reality had arrived with three-axle force. The truck, hauling a long trailer, turned onto that unimproved road and idled right under the windows of my mother's second-floor living space.

On the trailer was a large machine with a great steel arm stretching to the taillights. As the truck lumbered up the lane where I walked the dogs every day, I saw the business end of that arm and knew the purpose of that huge, serrated disc: cut down everything in its path.

Greater sadness accompanied this second logging operation. Not only were we now familiar with the devastation that would follow the clear-cut, but it was happening during summertime. Birds, fawns, fox, bears, insects, wildflowers, squirrels, and bees already had made homes in those imminently endangered woods. Every field, wood, fallen tree, and brook is a busy ecosystem during the summer. That serrated monster impacted much more than a deer yard.

German poet, painter, and novelist Herman Hesse had this to say about the purpose of trees: "Trees are sanctuaries. Whoever knows how to speak to them, whoever knows how to listen to them, can learn the truth. They do not preach learning and precepts; they preach, undeterred by particulars, the ancient law of life." And yet humans, who are non-tree entities, do not respect the ancient law of life. We act as if we are superior to trees, animals, insects, and amphibians. As if the life of a human is more valuable than the life of a tree. What is this human compulsion to dominate, desecrate, and destroy? We seem utterly unable to live in harmony with nature, insistent that our needs trump any ecosystem, any lesson from the past, or any consideration of the future.

As the truck disappeared into the lush, green, unsuspecting woods behind our home, I grabbed my yoga mat and rolled it out on the deck at the south end of the house that is shaded by two twenty-year-old maple trees. I stood there, breathing in and out. I looked at what was always in front of me, around me, and above me: trees. These trees create oxygen out of the carbon dioxide we breathe out. They clean the air we breathe in. As I stood there, consciously breathing in peace and breathing out my anger, the maple trees took that exhale, that anger, and absorbed it.

One mature leafy tree, like the ones at the south end of our home, produces enough oxygen for ten people. Within two weeks, the woodlot behind our house would be flattened; two weeks to decimate what took fifty years to grow. Doesn't that take your breath away?

Moving to the country and writing about rural life has introduced me to myriad people. Hearing stories from lifelong rural residents whose families have lived here for generations has awakened me to the reality that this is where we all began and this is where we all will end. This is where the barns are disappearing, leaving swallows and bats without homes. This is where we dump chemicals on the blueberry fields on the mountain without worrying about their impact downriver. This is where we level our woods in order to build and heat our homes, leaving birds and animals and insects without habitat, and leaving humans with fewer purifiers of the air that is polluted by the machines that cut down the trees in the first place.

We think air, water, and soil are ours to command and control and consume, but this is our human folly and it will be our downfall. We know how we hurt the environment, and ultimately ourselves, and we've known it for sixty, eighty, a hundred years. Yet we refuse to make the choices and the sacrifices that will make a difference: we buy powerboats instead of solar panels, camper trailers instead of personal windmills. We clear-cut because people want their cords of wood as cheap as possible. We buy meat packaged with foam trays and plastic wrap because it's convenient. We pollute the air, water, and soil because we believe we are invincible. We close our eyes and refuse to see what is right in front of us.

I'm as guilty as any consumer and any company that puts price and profit before that which provides us with everything: air, water, and soil. Standing on a deck of pressure-treated wood, on a rubber yoga mat, breathing in the scent of the grass my husband was cutting with a gas-powered, ride-on lawn mower, I took the only action an arrogant, all-consuming, doomed human being could: I put my palms together, bowed towards those mature leafy trees, and said, "Thank you. And, I'm sorry."

Within weeks, logging trucks began hauling the bodies of fallen trees away and I didn't dare count the number of loads that passed by the house. Why do we insist on calling forestry a renewable resource? If we are cutting trees down faster than they can grow, how can that be considered renewable? At the rate trees are being trucked out of Cumberland County, there will be a fifty-year gap between the land lying flat, covered only in the remains of the trees, and the regenerated woods ready to be cut down again. By then, it may be too late. Our losses will have overwhelmed us.

My husband has been logging woodlots since he was a young boy, first on his father's three hundred acres across the river and then on his own acreage. He, too, is concerned by the lack of mandatory replanting laws in Nova Scotia. He often speaks about Sweden, a country whose Forestry Act includes mandatory reforestation and a ban on felling young stands. He wonders why we don't do that in Nova Scotia.

He's not just talk, either; he has put money and effort behind his words. After cutting down the thirty-two-acre woodlot that borders the field directly behind his house, he had it replanted in black spruce because, even though it grows slowly, it grows well in low, wet land. Today, those trees are over ten years old and many are well over two metres tall.

Not only would my husband like the province to bring in a mandatory replanting law, he has his own idea for rebuilding our woods, which in turn invests in the future of our forestry industry, keeps rural land productive, and recreates habitats and oxygen-makers. He wants the government to invest in the old fields that no one is farming anymore: "The government would pay for the site prep, for the trees and for the planting," he explained to me. "Then the land owners, and the province, end up with all these fields that are growing a useful crop again. That means jobs and income for the next generation."

Not all those replanted woods would be cut down, either, so that means homes, food, and oxygen for the next generation of creatures—including humans. Without trees, none of us has a future. Besides, who knows whose souls will be running like sap through the trunks of those trees? My husband is thinking about his own future, as well.

8

More Power to Them

◦—————·•·—————◦

Driving along the winding one-kilometre lane running through the woods, you can imagine this drive is lovely in any season, even in winter. It's not a lane you'd want to have to plow, but the lack of roadside poles is a hint that perhaps that doesn't matter to the people who live here. There is no power where I'm headed. Well, there *is*, but it's not electric and it's more than solar.

When the woods open up, the view becomes panoramic. Debbie and Mike Cameron greet me on the wide front porch of their small, picturesque home along the shores of the Northumberland Strait.

"We'd been coming back here for several years in a tent trailer, from May to October," Debbie explains as we settle into comfortable chairs in the cozy living room, steaming mugs of tea in hand. "A tent trailer isn't really designed for that kind of use so it was getting the crap kicked out of it. We were thinking of getting a serious fifth-wheel when Mike suggested we put up a small cottage."

At the time, the couple was living in a 2,600-square-foot log house they'd built themselves on Tatamagouche Mountain. They wanted to downsize to a simple cottage on their one-acre stretch of beach. They planned for 600 square feet, completely off the grid.

"Even if there was a power pole installed right over there tomorrow," says Debbie, "we still wouldn't hook up. We made a conscious choice to be off-grid. We built it as a cottage and never intended to live here [year-round]. We had solar panels but not as many as we do now."

In fact, they weathered Hurricane Juan safely and comfortably in their cottage while their on-grid neighbours had to cope without power for a couple of days.

Looking back, that storm marked the start of a journey they never expected to embark upon, but one lined with three large road signs they could not ignore.

A year after they built their cottage, Debbie spent two weeks in Guatemala as part of an "active presence" with the Maritime Breaking the Silence Network, a group of volunteers created in 1988 to show support and solidarity for citizens of that country after the genocide by the Guatemalan army against Mayan communities and social activists. It was a perspective-changing experience for Debbie.

"It made me aware of how fortunate we are," she says. "The biggest learning experience for me was that they weren't asking for everything that we have, for us to give up everything we have. They were asking us to share; we don't need to have everything while they have nothing."

Debbie's group happened to be in a village on the day the locals held a ceremony for the opening of their new well. When she saw the circumstances and the size of the community well, she realized how precious water was as a commodity.

"I saw women who had one pot of water [to last] the day. What would they do? Cook with it or wash their kids? Imagine making that choice every day," she marvelled. "The women have headaches from not drinking enough water. Here in Canada, we use fresh water to flush our toilets."

The next sign appeared when Mike, an electrician, took a job with the salt mine in Pugwash; the cottage was only five minutes away compared to the thirty-minute commute from Tatamagouche Mountain. The couple began considering a change of residence.

But the biggest sign, one they couldn't ignore, finally came during a vacation in 2008. Debbie calls it her epiphany: "We were sailing with Mike's relatives through the Gulf Islands off BC," she explains. "They live on their boat and they were so happy and free and liberated and I basically had a meltdown [saying], 'I don't want my house, I don't want my cottage.' Something had to go. I was so overwhelmed." Debbie sips her tea as she tries to find a way to explain the juxtaposition. "I lived for the house [on Tatamagouche Mountain]. It was a log house that we'd built ourselves as newlyweds. It was unique and it became our identity. Our home and our lifestyle became our identity. Now I had a house and a cottage and I knew I didn't want to take care of both. I was never happy trying to be in both those places."

Since they enjoyed life at the cottage and it had proven its worth and toughness during Hurricane Juan, Debbie and Mike decided to fully embrace an off-the-grid lifestyle. According to Debbie, the hardest part wasn't selling the house but responding to the reaction of people when she told them what they were doing.

"When you make an internal decision to make a change, you've processed it, but when I blurted out to people that we were going to sell the house, people couldn't get over what we were walking away from. But for us, the beach won."

Debbie knew the challenge would be making the small space functional, and with that came the gut-wrenching task of letting go of all the stuff she'd accumulated over twenty-five years.

"We've had people tell us we've done what they've always dreamed of doing, but may not ever be able to face: that total letting go of so many material things. I discovered that what used to seem sacred all of a sudden could go in the yard sale."

Debbie and Mike moved from a large, two-storey home with a finished basement to a 600-square-foot one-level home with one bedroom and a loft for their grandchildren. (Now married forty years, they have two children and five grandchildren.) Another small room provides a space for storage and the washing machine (no dryer). They turned their son's motorcycle shed into a guest bunkie. Everything is beautifully decorated. One of Debbie's talents is decorating; an extension of her gardening and artistic skills.

"Instead of having to maintain a huge house, I can now focus on my gardens, on my art, and on reading," Debbie says. Another benefit of downsizing.

She admits the close quarters aren't for everyone and she misses having her own space ("You really have to like the person you're living with"), but it's all been worth it for the Camerons. Besides, there are acres upon acres of beach and forest to explore if things get too cramped indoors. They are also planning to add on another room.

When it comes to the technical part of their off-the-grid lifestyle, Mike's skills are invaluable (although it is a bit ironic that an electrician would choose to live without electricity). Expanding the cottage's existing solar system to take on more systems was Mike's special challenge. His electrical training allowed him to do much of the work himself, and means he's able to explain the whole system in a way anyone can understand.

"We have four deep-cycle batteries and those batteries are charged by solar panels and a small wind turbine. Off the batteries we have an inverter that changes DC voltage to AC voltage. That's 12 volts to 120. That runs any 120-volt appliances we have: satellite TV, washing machine, fridge, and deep freeze. Everything else is 12 volt: our lights, the water pump."

Mike explains Debbie doesn't use a hair dryer anymore because it uses so much energy, he'd have to hook up the generator.

"We have a back-up furnace that runs on propane," Mike goes on to say. "Our furnace and our hot water tank are RV-style. Our full-size range is propane. Our main source of heat is wood; we have a fireplace that heats the entire house in the wintertime."

There is a small wind turbine in the yard but Mike prefers solar over wind power.

"The turbine is more of a bonus to pick up wind at night," he says. "The solar panels work great. We do have a generator for backup if we get too many cloudy days in a row. We're probably good for four or five days if there is no sun. Solar panels still work when there is no sun, they're just not as efficient."

Their former house netted an annual power bill of about $3,000. Setting up the energy system at the cottage-turned-permanent-residence was a one-time cost of $7,000.

"Of course, the bigger the home and the more you want to run, the price is going to go up," Mike says, estimating the average home (running several 240-volt appliances) would cost about $20,000 to convert to a solar panel system.

"Everyone seems to think we're doing *without* something," Debbie says, "so I say, tell me what it is that we're going without: we have lights, satellite TV, refrigeration, the internet, and cellphones. We have everything we need; we just don't have to pay Nova Scotia Power anything. There is a savings but even if there wasn't, it's still nice to outsmart a monopoly."

For Debbie, the greatest satisfaction comes from putting words into action.

"Gandhi said, 'be the example of what you want to see in the world,' so it's about living simply and for us, that happens at the beach. You can just as easily do that in a six-hundred-square-foot house on the mountain. We have the life that we want and we are trying to be the example that you can be happy without having six bathrooms in your house."

Or flushing away fresh, clean water.

"The composting toilet is awesome," Debbie grins. "We don't have a septic, just a drainage field for grey water. There's less smell than a traditional toilet. It's all in the way it's vented and the air circulates and the drum rotates. And at some point, everything that is produced inside that toilet ends up spread around the rose bushes."

She laughs because visitors always compliment her on her beautiful roses.

Just in case you're thinking you could never manage the way Mike and Debbie do, think of the one thing you wouldn't want to give up, the hardest item to part with if you had to downsize, and remember this: Debbie has forty-seven boxes of books stacked in an outbuilding. She loves her composting toilet and her 12-volt lights but she loves books just as much.

There is one other part of this story that has come full circle since Debbie's big epiphany eight years ago. Although Mike is still a few years from retirement, Debbie says they have already realized another dream: they now have their own thirty-foot sailboat. Like downsizing, there seemed to be signs pointing them in the direction of buying this sailboat: it was built in 1975, the year they married, and its name is *From Away*, the name of the gift shop Debbie worked in at the time.

"People associate boats with wealth but you couldn't buy a car for what we paid for the boat," she says. "We have arrived, but it's on our terms."

9

The Inevitable End
of Summer

⸺ ⋅∶⋅ ⸺

At ten o'clock in the morning, the chairs on the front deck sit in the shade. A month ago, you couldn't sit there on sunny days for the oppressive heat, but now the cat is curled up in one of those chairs on a yellow towel laid down earlier to soak up the heavy dew. She will nap in cool comfort until the sun moves out from behind the leafy branches of the vast Manitoba maple.

A change in the sun. Heavy dew. Comfortable rest. It must be August.

The sun hangs lower in the sky now and it doesn't take a glance through *The Farmer's Almanac* to know summer is slipping away. Blue herons gather along the shore in the outer basin of Pugwash Harbour and this year's osprey hatchlings have left their nest, building strength and learning to fish in advance of next month's migration south. The sunflowers and rudbeckia wave their deep yellow blossoms as the day lilies finally die out and the wild asters around the chicken coop raise their fuzzy purple faces towards the drooping sun.

When I step into my husband's garage, where he is changing blades on the lawn mower for the last time this season, I stop and listen.

"Your pet cricket is chirping," I say to him.

For the last week or so, every time I've walked in here I hear a cricket (and simply assume it's the same one). It reminds me of the cottage my family had when I was a child, a large open concept cottage with no ceilings, just wide-open rafters. We could set our watches by the late-summer serenade of a cricket at eight o'clock every evening: the song of the sunset.

'Tis the season for crickets: we had two large ones where I worked in town and their sudden appearance this time of year remains a mystery. Then again, maybe not: the one-storey building was once a gas station, and converted into the local newspaper office in the 1950s. The outline of the original double garage doors is still evident in the brickwork, and gaps exist that only crickets know about—like secret passageways running behind the walls of a castle—and daily our office was serenaded by this pair.

Through research, I learn it is only the male cricket that chirps. Inside my husband's garage, perhaps this is the pet cricket's last-ditch effort to find a female companion as the dew coats the grass and the night air cools the ground. "It's more comfortable in here, my sweet," he might be chirping. "Come in and we'll overwinter behind the woodpile."

In his book about the salt marsh behind his home, biologist, writer, and Tidnish Bridge resident Harry Thurston opens his chapter on August thusly: "During the cricket-enchanted days of August I often sit on the dock." I find it the most perfect sentiment because this is what I do during August; I slow down and sit more often at the water or on the deck, knowing the yellow of these warm, dry summer days is slowly transforming into the orange and red of autumn.

Beauty fading to brilliance.

If the chirp of a lonely male cricket is the way August sounds, this is how it smells: golden and spicy. In a quiet hurricane season, August is hot and dry, yet swollen with the culmination of all that is summer. It is when we try to cram every last summer moment into the ever-loosening days and the star-blazing nights. August reflects our urge to gather and enjoy everything—morning coffee, afternoon iced tea, evening barbecues—to the fullest. It is the month of harvest; when the labour and hope of the rainy days of early June, and the constant watering and weeding of mid-July produce an abundance of dazzling flowers and luscious vegetables.

Vegetable gardens provided intriguing interludes throughout my childhood. My clearest memories are these: Skipping under the long arbour of raspberry canes in the yard of my father's relatives, Frank and Minnie George; standing on the bottom slat of the white fence surrounding my grandfather's huge, well-tended garden; and watching my great-uncle Everett in his straw hat stooped over in his garden at his cottage in Coboconk, Ontario.

It might be possible to have a late-onset genetic disposition to have a vegetable garden, a hankering stirred by my return to Nova Scotia when I was thirty-two years old. I'd just spent the entire summer at my parents' vacation home in Pugwash after more than five years in Vancouver and in early September, I was reading Barbara Kingsolver's novel *Prodigal Summer*; a thick, lush book about three people living in the southern Appalachian Mountains. Sitting on the front deck of our summer house surrounded by farm fields and overlooking the Pugwash harbour, I wrote in my notebook about how good I was feeling:

> *It's the fresh air but it's also the pungent stench of manure in that fresh air. I feel alive here, in tune with natural rhythms, connected to the seasons. I think I can even feel the rotation of the earth. I used to live a block away from a grocery store, a bookstore, a movie rental store, a dozen restaurants, a dozen coffee shops and yet here, on this dead-end rural road, I feel like part of the world. There's life, there's death, there's mating*

and birth, there's planting and growing and harvesting. The longer I am here, the more I want to grow my own food, raise goats, and keep chickens. The ritual and routine of country life suits me, settles me. Is it autumn that makes me feel ripe and content like an apple tree heavy with red fruit? I have this urge to make green tomato relish.

It took another five years before I could put these wishes into practice, when that ripe contentment I was oozing attracted the notice of a Nova Scotia country boy who happened to have a large property, a hankering for chickens, and a love of growing his own vegetables. And so it happened that after all those gardens of my childhood—when I was entrusted with shelling and peeling, never planting or weeding—I dug up a potato for the first time at the age of thirty-seven.

The vegetable garden was entirely my husband's domain because my early attempts at picking carrots and beets yielded nothing but greens and the teeniest roots, so I stopped helping for fear of decimating his hard work. But surely, I thought, I could handle potatoes.

We'd been eating new potatoes for weeks so I thought I could manage to harvest enough for supper before my husband arrived home from work. The first plant came out of the ground with a potato nub the size of my pinkie hanging off it. I pulled up another plant. Nothing. Not even a nubbin. I called the country boy at work.

"I want to get potatoes out of the garden before it rains," I explained, "but when I pull the plants up, there's nothing there."

A sigh wafted through the line. "They aren't like carrots and beets, dear. You take your little garden rake, that hand-held one you have, and dig around in the dirt. They should just come rolling out."

So, little rake in hand, I returned to the garden. I knelt down where I'd yanked out the first plant and stuck my rake into the dirt. One stroke. No potato. Another stroke. Out popped a lovely, round, yellow potato. Excitement bubbled up inside my throat and spurted out my mouth in a loud, giggling shriek like I was five years old: *look what I did all by myself!*

I raked some more and two more potatoes popped out of the soil. I was digging potatoes! There I was, kneeling in a garden near a river in rural Nova Scotia, digging potatoes out of the fresh earth to take them inside, wash them off, and boil them for supper.

In 1959, John Updike wrote a poem entitled "Hoeing," in which he expresses his fear that the younger generation will not know the pleasure and importance of the task. The poem closes with these lines: "Ignorant the wise boy who/has never performed this simple, stupid and useful wonder." Ignorant the wise girl who has never dug potatoes.

I continue to grow in wisdom and confidence since those two first summers. Every time I walk across our yard to the garden to pick vegetables for supper and the late-afternoon sun warms my skin, I want to stop, hold onto this month with both hands, slow it down, capture the lazy ripeness of August, and make it last a little longer than thirty-one golden days.

For these are the last days to harvest the little jewels we long for when the snows of February pile up: the joy of discovering and reclaiming old ways, the appreciation of harvesting our own food, and the unique and irreplaceable lushness of rural life during the enchanted days of August.

10

Recipe for a Maritime Dinner Party

⌒————·•·————⌒

In the summer of 1979, my family of four arrived in Nova Scotia for the first time on the invitation of our minister, Garth, back in Ontario. He wanted us to see where he'd grown up: a very small place called Pugwash about an hour from the New Brunswick border.

We drove through the village, then out along the then-gravel Pugwash Point Road, and made the slow journey across a number of pastures. We had to stop every so often to get out of the car, unlatch a wooden gate, drive the car through, and then re-latch the gate. I can still feel the excitement and wonder as we marvelled at the red gravel road and the red soil.

Finally, we reached a brown cabin perched on the edge of the cliff overlooking the Northumberland Strait. The cabin had a huge window overlooking the water, three bedrooms where we spent as little time as possible, no electricity, and no running water. Propane lights, an outhouse perched partway down the cliff, and a hand water pump solved those issues.

I was a nine-year-old kid and not perturbed by any of that. It was different, but I'd grown up with family cottages so outhouses weren't new to me. Getting water from the outdoor pump was only a problem because I wasn't quite strong enough to get it primed myself. The only negative part of the trip I remember was the jellyfish in the water.

Raised in southern Ontario on lakes that did not rise and lower every twelve hours, my sister and I had no notion of tides. So on a warm August afternoon as we played on a sandbar, we failed to notice our shrinking real estate.

"Come in, come in!" Garth shouted from far above our heads.

A wide ribbon of water had appeared between the shore and our diminishing sandbar. Our fear of being stung by the jellyfish paralyzed us. I was sure Garth would clamber down and get into the rowboat to save us, but he stayed up on the cliff, shouting and waving his arms. My sister looked at me and I grabbed her hand. Quickly but carefully, we picked our way across seaweed-slick rocks through the deepening water until we reached the shore, safe from the jellies and tide swallowing up the sandbar.

Honestly, outside of that crystal-clear recollection, my memories of that summer are hazy, the way childhood memories become over thirty or forty years, fading and disintegrating, leaving only the sense of wonderful or awful. When it comes to specifics—what the water felt like, how often we swam, what we ate, or even how we passed the days—I just remember the feeling: it was magical.

It wasn't our only trip that summer (we also went to Niagara Falls), so my mother put together a special photo album for the summer of 1979; many of my memories come alive through those images. Since we returned to Pugwash year after year after year, my memories have been supplanted by scary movies, first kisses, lobster suppers, sulky races, a kitten from the barn down the road, cows lining up along the fence, and—most poignantly—my father's final best years after he was diagnosed with Alzheimer's disease.

My father had been in the nursing home for six months and my mother had just had surgery to remove cancer from her body when she sent me to the house on Pugwash Point in the summer of 2006.

"You should go to Pugwash. Take the dogs and go."

"I'm not leaving you."

"I'm doing really well and I'm fine here. I want to be with your father."

Then my friend Diana phoned to say she had cancer, too, and would undergo surgery shortly. I packed up the van with two dogs and enough supplies for a month, hugged my mother goodbye, and made the eighteen-hour road trip to Nova Scotia.

It was almost like I'd had amnesia: I woke up on my first morning in the house on Pugwash Point. Diana and I walked the dogs on the beach. I ate breakfast in the dining room overlooking the harbour. I went to yoga then gathered with those friends on the front porch of the café for tea and coffee. It was as if I'd awakened in the place I'd always been—I just didn't remember the two and a half months leading up to that day.

The day before she'd gone in for her own surgery a few months earlier, my mother had given me a silver pendant with the word "laugh" stamped onto it. Of all the inspirational items she could have given me, this was a strange one. Given the circumstances, it seemed rather inappropriate. I thanked her for it nonetheless and wore it even though I couldn't figure out what she thought I'd be laughing at while taking care of two ill parents. The only reason I could come up with was that my mother enjoyed a good laugh. A hot bath or a good laugh were her ideas of restorative medicine.

No longer our ministers but still our lifelong friends, Garth and Dorothy Mundle were already at their cabin on the cliff on the back shore (now moved back from the eroding cliff and painted yellow), so they invited me over for supper. They were celebrating with their two grandchildren, and a pair of long-time friends who had been part of my family's very first trip east in 1979. Serendipity!

Okay, Mum, now I understand.

Here I was "on retreat" before my mother started her chemotherapy, providing some sort of support for my friend Diana (who had made it through her surgery just fine) taking my father's thirteen-year-old dog (who also had cancer) to the beach every morning, and I was laughing. I was having dinner with four people who had known me all my life and we were reminiscing and telling new stories and laughing.

It was exactly what I needed. For myself, for my mother, for Diana, for the future. Whatever it held, I was making new memories of sunshine and laughter, of lightheartedness and happiness, in case there were dark days of worry and dread to come.

When I woke up the next morning, this "recipe" wanted to be written down. It's a recipe for serving guests who have arrived from out of town, or "away," and want—but really, need—to experience the magic of a Maritime dinner party:

> Start with a warm, dry evening in late July.
> Invite several guests to your plumbing-/water-/electricity-free cabin perched on the edge of a high cliff overlooking a wide expanse of water with a view of Prince Edward Island.
> Make sure these guests haven't visited this place since 1979.
> Send guests down rickety wooden stairs to the beach for a refreshing swim with the jellyfish.
> Soak in brine for 15 to 20 minutes.
> Begin marinating by serving gin and tonics and sour apple martinis in large plastic tumblers. Watch as guests mellow and forget there is no running water.
> Invite guests to join you at the picnic table outside near the high cliff overlooking the wide expanse of water. Ask guests to work around the large sandstone rocks holding down the tablecloth. Point out three deer in the field next to the cabin.
> Tell them that's what they're having for dinner.
> Pour red wine into glasses. When only one guest wants white wine, serve it to him in a small beer stein. Watch as guests mellow even more and forget there is an outhouse.

> Serve 10 pounds of mussels in a huge steel bowl. Provide melted butter and hot whole-wheat buns. Listen to the click and clatter of empty shells as well as exclamations of delight and groans of pleasure. Note how conversation comes to a halt.
> Bring guests inside the cabin for the main course. In honour of the two children present, sing grace.
> Marvel at the eight different keys in which grace was sung.
> Serve heaps of breaded scallops, boiled new potatoes, and fresh green beans. Make sure all wine glasses (and the stein) are topped up. Watch the continued mellowing of guests who forget your cabin is located on the side of a high cliff overlooking a wide expanse of water.
> Clear main course dishes before serving tea and coffee and a sour cherry pie for dessert. Inform guests that no one needs ice cream with a pie made with Maritime sour cherries. Don't remind them it's really because there is no electricity and no freezer in which to store ice cream anyway.
> To provide one last helping of memories: go outside and build a bonfire. Watch the guests reach full mellow-oration and forget that it has been thirty years since they last visited (and wonder why it took them thirty years to return).
> Look up at the vast black sky full of stars and discuss quantum physics.

Serves: 8
Can be refrigerated and stored forever.

Acknowledgements

My mother says the only person who really needs to be thanked is her...
sorry, Mother, you're wrong (again).

On the professional side, my thanks to Charlie Weeks and the late
Paul Marchant of the *Oxford Journal* who gave the "Field Notes" column its
start; Darrell Cole at the *Citizen-Record*; Jim and Linda Gourlay, Heather
White, and Jodi DeLong of *Saltscapes* magazine; and Paul O'Connell and
Colleen Cosgrove at the *Chronicle-Herald*. Special thanks to fellow writers
Harry Thurston, Monica Graham, and Deanne Fitzpatrick for their wisdom
and encouragement. I am delighted to be part of the Nimbus family. Thank
you to Whitney Moran for saying yes, and to Emily MacKinnon for being
an amazing editor.

On the personal side, my deepest thanks to Jane, Christina, Mary P.,
Elaine, Sarah, Jennifer, Janice, Kerry, Kim, Judy, Harold, and Shelagh for
being such wonderful friends; to everyone in the Mundle clan: I wouldn't
be where I am today without you; to the church friends who have welcomed
me so warmly; and to my in-laws for being genuinely pleased to have me as
a daughter-in-law. To everyone who is named in this book, I am grateful for
and blessed by your contribution and willingness to let me share your story
with others. My gratitude also to Johnny Reid, who provided an amazing
soundtrack for my adventures in rural living.

Thank you Kim Malonie, animal communicator, for listening to Stella
and helping me understand her. She was part of my urban and rural lives
for twelve years and I will never walk as many miles with a dog as I did with
her. We buried Stella under an oak tree in the field she loved to wander.

I am grateful to my father for instilling in me a love of nature. I wish he
could have been a greater part of this adventure: he would have loved it.

Dwayne, you are my heart and my home. Thank you for your unflagging belief that I could do this.

And finally, everything begins and ends with you, Mother. It seemed
like a good idea at the time and turned out just fine. Love you. Thank you.
Lunch is on me. (I mean it this time.)